REPORTING ON RISK

REPORTING ON RISK

*How the Mass Media Portray Accidents,
Diseases, Disasters, and Other Hazards*

Eleanor Singer and Phyllis M. Endreny

RUSSELL SAGE FOUNDATION   /   NEW YORK

The Russell Sage Foundation

The Russell Sage Foundation, one of the oldest of America's general purpose foundations, was established in 1907 by Mrs. Margaret Olivia Sage for "the improvement of social and living conditions in the United States." The Foundation seeks to fulfill this mandate by fostering the development and dissemination of knowledge about the country's political, social, and economic problems. While the Foundation endeavors to assure the accuracy and objectivity of each book it publishes, the conclusions and interpretations in Russell Sage Foundation publications are those of the authors and not of the Foundation, its Trustees, or its staff. Publication by Russell Sage, therefore, does not imply Foundation endorsement.

Library of Congress Cataloging-in-Publication Data

Singer, Eleanor.
   Reporting on risk / Eleanor Singer, Phyllis M. Endreny.
     p.   cm.
   Includes bibliographical references and index.
   ISBN 0-87154-801-1
   1. Disasters in the press. 2. Reporters and reporting.
3. Television broadcasting of news. 4. Risk. I. Endreny, Phyllis M.
(Phyllis Mildred), 1944–   . II. Title.
PN4784.D57S56   1993
070.4′49904—dc20   92-40130
                                                                      CIP

RUSSELL SAGE FOUNDATION
112 East 64th Street, New York, New York 10021

10 9 8 7 6 5 4 3 2 1

Contents

To Our Families for Their Loving Support

Acknowledgments

This book owes its existence to many generous supporters. Foremost, of course, is the Russell Sage Foundation, which funded the project in 1984. In particular, the encouragement and confidence of our project officer, Peter de Janosi, were crucial to the initial research and, later, to the writing of the book. Two semester-long fellowships at the Gannett Center for Media Studies at Columbia University, now known as the Freedom Forum Media Studies Center, provided the senior author with the leisure and research assistance to undertake the analysis of the data. We are grateful to Everette E. Dennis for providing an environment extraordinarily supportive of research and writing. And, finally, an invitation from Peter Mohler to come to ZUMA as a visiting professor in the summer of 1991, together with the colleagueship of Hans-Juergen Hippler and Norbert Schwarz there, provided the impetus for the final rewriting of the manuscript. To Peter Strauss, good friend, we are indebted for sustained encouragement and wise counsel. The second author wishes to express her profound gratitude to her siblings, Corinne E. Kirchner and Ray G. Endreny;

their generous support and sustenance of all kinds has been meaningful beyond words and measure.

The work itself would not have been possible without the contribution of a series of dedicated and competent coders and research assistants, who are listed here in alphabetical order: Nuna Alberts, Lisa DelCompare, Laura Elwyn, and Anastasios Kalomiris. The statistical consultation and collegial support of Marc Glassman were indispensable throughout the project's duration, right up until the last days of revision and checking.

Three of the chapters that comprise the book appeared in somewhat different form as articles in the *Journal of Communication* and *Journalism Quarterly*. We are grateful to the editors and reviewers of those journals for their very helpful and constructive criticisms of those chapters.

The process of collaboration is never easy, and often strains the quality of the relationship beyond the breaking point. Though we have had our share of strains, we are happy to say our friendship has endured through what proved to be a longer gestation period than anybody involved with this book had bargained for.

ELEANOR SINGER
PHYLLIS M. ENDRENY
New York, May 1992

1 / Why Look at the Reporting of Risk?

On April 2, 1986, when a suspected terrorist bomb exploded inside a TWA jet over Greece, killing four Americans, the *New York Times* printed a front-page story by Ralph Blumenthal titled, "On Terrorism and Tourism: Americans Alter Travel Plans." In it, Blumenthal reported on the decline in American travel to several countries in Europe and the Middle East. Four paragraphs into the story, he noted the decline in the value of the dollar and, in the following paragraph, commented: "It is difficult to measure the relative impact of terrorism against the declining dollar. But the reports make clear that terrorism is casting a long shadow over tourism this year." And the spate of articles on cutbacks in tourism that followed the midair explosion all emphasized the role played by the fear of terrorism.

In a subsequent column (April 22), Tom Wicker of the *Times* tried to put the risks posed by terrorism into perspective. "Americans," he pointed out, "are not in the habit of canceling vacation trips by automobile because of the high incidence of highway accidents—a substantially greater threat to most of them than the terrorist's bomb. In fact, *Newsweek* magazine reports that more

Americans drowned in the bathtub last year than were killed in terrorist attacks."

But there is abundant evidence that individuals confronted with risky choices do not behave in accordance with purely rational calculations of benefits and costs (Tversky and Kahneman, 1974, 1981; Kahneman and Tversky, 1982). Research on the factors that influence such choices has so far emphasized primarily psychological considerations, with less attention to the social influences that shape the perception of risk.[1]

Yet Kahneman and Tversky (1982) have hinted at the profound effect which social definitions have by noting that it is possible greatly to increase the probability with which a specific cost-benefit ratio is chosen by labeling it "insurance." Apparently, it is the social, rather than the mathematical, definition of risk that influences choice.

But where do these social definitions come from? Most perceptions of risk are mediated by one of three sources: personal experience; direct contact with other people; and indirect contact, by way of the mass media. This is a study of the third source of influence. It analyzes the reporting of risks in the nonfictional mass media in order to gain some insight into how such reporting shapes individuals' assessment of the risks present in their environment.[2]

Most people do not think continually about the likelihood of accident, injury, disease, and death, either to themselves or to those close to them. For the most part, we attend to such risks very selectively. Preparing to travel abroad, we do not ordinarily think about the possibility of a terrorist attack. We are even less likely to worry about the risk of a derailment when getting into a subway car, or about catching Legionnaire's disease on vacation.

Under certain circumstances, however, some of these risks to life and health become more salient than they had previously been, and this in turn may alter the perception of their relative frequency and, potentially, alter behavior in relation to them.

---

[1] But see Johnson and Covello (1987) for some analyses of such social factors.

[2] Two classic studies of panic behavior following radio broadcasts of fictitious disasters—Cantril's *Invasion from Mars* (1940) and Rosengren's "Barseback 'Panic'" (1974)—attest to the power of the media to shape such perceptions, at least under certain conditions. Nevertheless, fictional accounts have been excluded from the present study.

Having been trapped for several hours in a malfunctioning elevator, one may be more inclined to walk up and down stairs—for a while, and for a reasonable number of flights. Hearing about a friend's robbery, one may decide to install a burglar alarm.

These examples, quite deliberately, emphasize personal experience, or vicarious experience through one's acquaintances or friends. But for certain classes of events, information about risk is likely to come neither from personal experience nor from any other interpersonal source but, rather, from the symbolic environment of the mass media. Surveys in the United States, for example, show that in 1991 only 15–20 percent of the population personally knew anyone who was ill with AIDS (Acquired Immune Deficiency Syndrome), but more than 99 percent had heard or read about Magic Johnson's decision to quit professional basketball because he had tested positive for the AIDS virus (*Los Angeles Times* survey, November 21–24, 1991). Or, to take another example, within a half hour of the space shuttle *Challenger's* explosion on January 28, 1986, 69 percent of American adults had learned about the disaster, according to a survey by R. H. Bruskin. Of these, 58 percent named either television or radio as their first source of information (Television Information Office, "Quick Takes from TIO," No. 2, May 1986). And in Switzerland, where fewer than 100 people were killed in 1985 as a result of all categories of criminal acts, including murder, a 1986 poll found that 55 percent of the women surveyed feared going out alone at night. Writing in the *New York Times* on August 5, 1986 ("Disappearance of a Child Fuels Swiss Fear of Crime"), Thomas W. Nettler quoted public officials as saying that the rate of criminal attacks had been stable in Switzerland for several years, and that the number of reported rapes and sexual assaults had actually declined, from 391 in 1984 to 365 in 1985. But Nettler pointed out that Swiss state television, as well as several popular magazines, had given extensive coverage to a cluster of recent kidnappings and two sexual assaults and murders, and noted: "The authorities say the appearance of danger in Switzerland may have been magnified by the publicity surrounding the recent cases."

These examples suggest that knowledge about, and even attitudes toward, certain kinds of hazards are influenced by their coverage in the press. What is the nature of the hazards to life and health whose perception is likely to be mediated in this way? In the first place, such hazards are likely to be *serious*—that is, the probability of associated death or disability is high. And second, the probability that such a hazard will occur at all is likely to be quite *small*.

Putting this another way, such risky events are likely to be regarded as "newsworthy" by journalistic standards, and therefore to be reported in the press. Reporting, in turn, is likely to make such events more readily available to attention and recall. In fact, in a study of the role of interpersonal and mass media channels in public awareness and comprehension of major news stories, Robinson and Levy (1986) found that the news stories most likely to be recalled were those involving especially dramatic news of real or potential danger. And the result of such increased salience is likely to be an increased perception of risk—especially because, as we show later, the media provide very little direct information about the risks associated with different types of hazards. Instead, the public is left to infer the extent of danger from the amount and prominence of the coverage a hazard receives.

SOME THEORIES ABOUT MEDIA EFFECTS

The hypothesis that the media influence perceptions of risk is only a specific instance of a more general theory about the effects of the media on cognitions and attitudes.

The more limited form of this theory is known as "agenda-setting" (Cohen, 1963; McCombs and Shaw, 1972), and specifies that while the media may not be able to affect *what* we think, they are very successful in telling us what to think about—that is, in making certain issues or events more salient or significant. In an early study, for example, Funkhouser (1973) showed that the perception of the "most important problem facing America" was more closely correlated with measures of the amount of media coverage than with more "objective" measures of social problems—for example, crime rates or numbers of racial disturbances. And Zucker (1978) showed that agenda-setting effects were most likely to occur for unobtrusive issues—that is, those that generally lie outside of the individual's personal experience and for which, therefore, the media provide virtually the only frame of reference (cf. also Johnson and Covello, 1987: 179–80).[3]

The stronger version of the theory of media effects is known as "cultivation theory" (cf. Gerbner and Gross, 1976; Gerbner et al., 1977). This theory attributes to media—specifically, television—distinctive attitudinal and cognitive effects. Describing the world of fictional television as filled with violence, for example, Gerbner and his colleagues hypothesize that habitual viewing of such a world will "cultivate" a certain perspective on the part of heavy viewers, who will come to see the world as a more violent place than it really is and will exhibit more fearfulness and related characteristics than light viewers in similar circumstances. Although Gerbner's research has aroused considerable controversy and criticism (see, e.g., Hirsch, 1980, 1981; Hughes, 1980), in somewhat modified form it appears able to withstand such critical attacks (cf. T. Cook, Kendzierski, and Thomas, 1983). More recently, Kasperson and his colleagues (1988) have advanced a "conceptual framework" to account for the "amplification" of risks in the process of communicating them to the public.

Research based on cultivation theory deals with television drama, not real-life events. But several studies directly link the reporting of nonfictional hazards and their perception by the public. Combs and Slovic (1979), for example, correlated the frequency with which forty-one causes of death (i.e., "hazards") were reported in two small-town newspapers with estimates of the frequency of these same causes of death given by a group of students. The correlations were moderately high, and persisted even when the actual frequency of death associated with these causes was held constant.

Even stronger evidence comes from studies like that by Freimuth and Van Nevel (1981), which relates *changes* in the awareness of risks associated with asbestos exposure to increased coverage of asbestos-related risks resulting from a publicity campaign. The study examines independent and presumably equivalent samples for trends in knowledge and awareness, interpreting

[3]There is a very large literature on agenda-setting effects; for reviews, see Winter, 1981; Becker, 1982; Eyal, 1981, 1982; Graber, 1982; Weaver, 1982; Iyengar and Kinder, 1987; Rogers and Dearing, 1988; Protess and McCombs, 1991.

small increases in both as reflecting the increased coverage given to the issue by the media.

A variety of similar studies link reporting and risk-related attitudes or behavior. Singer, Rogers, and Glassman (1991), for example, interpret the increase in condom sales and in reported condom use between 1988 and 1989 as reflecting the effect of the 1988 government information campaign about AIDS. And Jones, Beniger, and Westoff (1980) found small effects on the reported discontinuation of birth control pills and intrauterine devices between 1970 and 1975 as a result of media coverage of negative publicity surrounding these two contraceptive methods. Several studies have linked media coverage of the nuclear-reactor accident at Three Mile Island to changes in public opinion about a variety of issues involving nuclear energy (Mazur, 1981a, 1981b; Mitchell, 1980). Thus, both theory and research support the proposition that what the media report about a hazard influences public perceptions and even behavior in relation to that hazard (cf. also Wiegman, 1989).[4] At the same time, theory and research are far from being able to specify the size or limits of those effects with any precision.

HAZARDS AND RISKS

The discussion so far calls attention to the need to define key terms. *Risk*, as used in this book, refers to the probability of property damage, injury, illness, or death associated with a *hazard*. In the definition of a hazard, we follow Hohenemser and his colleagues (1983), who define hazards as "threats to humans and

---

[4]Public perceptions of *economic* risk are said to be similarly affected. For example, at a 1979 symposium honoring the economist George Katona, Nobel Laureate James Tobin noted that publication of the results of Katona's surveys of economic behavior may themselves influence such behavior: "For example," he said, "investment intention surveys, directly or as fed through macro-models, influence investment. More generally, the diffusion of economy-wide statistics, obsessively headlined by the press and interpreted by the specialized media, has made the economy a very different ball game from 25, 50, or 75 years ago." Herbert H. Hyman, "The Survey Research Center at the University of Michigan," unpublished ms.

In 1992, the media were full of stories about how the perception of stagnation in the economy discouraged consumer spending, and a National Public Radio broadcast of "All Things Considered" on February 5, 1992, examined the role of the press in fostering this perception. Not unexpectedly, the economists interviewed for the program divided almost evenly on whether the press created the extremely pessimistic climate of opinion prevailing at that time or merely reflected current economic reality.

what they value." Toxic waste, poverty, low-level radiation, salt, tampons, automobiles, hurricanes, malaria—all these are "hazards," as we use the term.

But the media rarely report on hazards, nor, except on the financial pages, do they report on "risks." They report, instead, on accidents, disasters, crime, new products, new surgical techniques, a food additive scare. In this study, we have translated the multitudinous reporting categories used by the media into a small number of general hazard categories, each of which subsumes a much larger number of specific hazards.

We distinguished seven basic types of hazard, only six of which are analyzed in detail in this book. The first of these is the category of "natural hazards."[5] This category includes events like hurricanes, blizzards, and volcanic eruptions, which are generally regarded as involving only "natural" forces, as well as famines, drought, and floods, which are often regarded as substantially man-made. In the analysis of the reporting of such hazards, we look specifically at who is held responsible for their occurrence.

The second category is that of "energy hazards," and includes what are often referred to as accidents—for example, airplane crashes, train wrecks, automobile accidents, fires. The list of specific energy hazards is drawn from Hohenemser et al. (1983), and is supplemented by additional energy hazards reported on during the period of our study. For example, amusement ride accidents, bus crashes, and helicopter crashes are energy hazards that we added to the list proposed by Hohenemser and his colleagues.

The third category of hazards includes what many people think of as technological risks, and are referred to by Hohenemser et al. (and by us) as "materials hazards." Among the hazards included in this category are asbestos, nuclear reactors, various chemicals, alcohol, and tobacco. Again, as with energy hazards, we supplemented the list provided by Hohenemser and his colleagues with additional hazards that surfaced in the media during the period of our study—e.g., methyl isocyanate (MIC), radon, and silicone implants.

In the scheme developed by Hohenemser and his colleagues,

---

[5]For a listing of all hazard categories as well as the specific hazards included under each, see Appendix A.

all known hazards can be grouped into the three categories just listed.[6] For our purposes, however, we adopted a somewhat more expansive—and less logically rigorous—system, which was better adapted to the way hazards are reported in the press. For example, we distinguished a fourth category, "activities involving benefits and costs," which includes such things as exercise, mountain climbing, jogging, and boxing. Viewed from a different perspective, these activities might have been included in the category of energy hazards (e.g., the hazard involved in mountain climbing is that of a fall, which Hohenemser et al. classify as an energy hazard). By the same token, some of the hazards that Hohenemser and his colleagues classify as materials hazards (e.g., alcohol, smoking) might easily have been classified by us as activities involving benefits and costs. The rule we adopted was to follow Hohenemser et al. when a particular hazard had already been categorized by them, and to follow the emphasis of the media source when it had not.

A similar looseness applies to our fifth category, that of chronic and acute illnesses. When the media focused on the *causes* of some of these illnesses (e.g., asbestos, cholesterol) we classified the resulting story as one involving a materials hazard. When, on the other hand, the story focused on the resulting illness (e.g., on cancer or heart disease) we classified the illness itself as the hazard.

The sixth category in our scheme is what we refer to as "complex technologies." These involve *clusters* of hazards, some technological, some social, that we have chosen to treat as single hazards rather than break them up into their constituent elements. They include surgery in general, as well as specific surgical procedures such as organ transplants. They also include euthanasia,

---

[6]Hohenemser et al. note that with a few exceptions, energy hazards "are distinguished by kinetic energy on a macroscopic scale, whereas materials hazards generally affect organisms on a molecular level. . . . Energy hazards have releases with short persistence times, averaging less than one minute; materials releases have long persistence times, averaging a week or more." Further, energy hazards have immediate consequences, whereas materials hazards have delayed consequences; energy hazards have effects restricted almost entirely to those exposed, whereas materials hazards often affect future generations; energy hazards have only insignificant effects on non-human mortality, whereas materials hazards afffect nonhumans as well as humans. For a discussion of these and other differences between the two categories of hazard, see Hohenemser et al. (1983).

inadequate medical care, and poverty. In many of these, the hazards arise more from imperfect social arrangements than from any technological defect.

The final category into which we classified media stories about hazards is one we dubbed "activities with costs only." This category includes conventional felony crimes as well as terrorist acts. Although most of these acts involve benefits for the perpetrators, they do not benefit their victims; hence the label, "activities with costs only." Because media coverage of these acts has been analyzed extensively by others, we have excluded them from the present study.

ISSUES IN THE REPORTING OF RISK

The present study differs from many other studies of hazards by focusing on the way they are reported in the mass media. It differs from other studies of hazard reporting because of its comparative perspective. Whereas other studies have tended to focus on one kind of hazard (e.g., Barton, 1969) or on one or two specific hazards (e.g., Mazur, 1981a; Mitchell, 1980; Nealey, Rankin, and Montano, 1978; Rankin and Nealey, 1979; Turner, Nigg, and Heller Paz, 1986), this study looks at the reporting of hundreds of different hazards in fifteen different media. As a result, we are able to compare the way natural hazards are reported with the way energy hazards are reported, for example, and also to compare print with television, and newspapers with newsmagazines. Furthermore, because we have built in a number of purposive comparisons, we can also see what difference the intended audience makes in the kinds of hazards selected for reporting, and we are able, as well, to look at changes in the reporting of hazards that have taken place over a period of twenty-four years, roughly a generation.

Of the many possible issues in risk reporting, we have chosen, in this book, to focus on four broad sets of questions that seem to us to be especially interesting from a social science perspective. They have to do with (1) the selection of hazards for coverage, (2) what information is provided about them, (3) responsibility for hazards and their prevention, and (4) accuracy of reporting. With respect to each of these, we are interested in (5) what variations exist among media. In this section, we discuss each of these issues in somewhat more detail.

Selection of Hazards for Coverage

In the first chapter of their book *Risk and Culture*, Douglas and Wildavsky (1982) raise the question of how social systems come to identify some risks and ignore others. They develop the thesis that "social principles . . . affect the judgment of what dangers should be most feared, what risks are worth taking, and who should be allowed to take them" (p. 6). "Whether blaming the elders or blaming the victim," they contend, "the type of society generates the type of accountability and focuses concern on particular dangers" (p. 7).[7]

In contemporary society, we believe the media both reflect and influence public perceptions of what constitutes a hazard and how serious the associated risks are. They do this both by selecting certain issues for attention, and by the kind of information they provide about them. As Nelkin (1985a:643) has put it in relation to the reporting of medical news:

> Through their selection . . . they set the agenda for public policy. Through their disclosure of medical discoveries they affect personal behavior. Through their style of presentation they lay the foundation for public attitudes and actions. Media coverage of medical events has implications for the distribution of scarce resources; access to the media can bring in research funds, and even body parts.

Or, as *Science* puts it in a more jocular vein:

> *Science:* Dr. Noitall, you are the ultimate world authority on all types of risks, a revered figure who has just appeared in [*sic*] national television.
> *Noitall:* A vast understatement of my true value.

[7]Though critics have challenged some aspects of Douglas and Wildavsky's argument, few have challenged their basic thesis, that societies selectively choose risks for attention, and that these choices are shaped by social and cultural considerations. Their perspective complements cognitive psychologists' theories of risk perception. Cf. Johnson and Covello (1987), pp. vii–x.

Science: You must have a large laboratory to uncover so many facts not available to the regulatory agencies.

Noitall: Facts are no longer created in laboratories, they are created by the media. Any pronouncement of mine repeated in three periodicals, four newspapers, or one television program is considered a fact. My appearance on three talk shows is enough to qualify me as an expert. It is no longer necessary to have a laboratory in my profession.[8]

One central question we address in this book, therefore, is the nature of the hazards the media select for attention. What are their characteristics? How do they come to be defined in this way?

One hypothesis about media attention to hazards is that such attention will fluctuate with changes in the "real world." Newly identified diseases, for example, will elicit a flurry of attention that then subsides, to be replaced by subsequent flurries as the disease spreads to new populations or areas, or as contributing factors, causes, or cures are identified.

Of course it is not only changes in the real world that drive these fluctuations but also the media's quest for "the new." Social scientists as well as others have decried journalists' tendency to "point with alarm" to the "crisis of the week," only to abandon that crisis, unresolved, at week's end (cf. Lawless, 1977).

But quite aside from variations that mirror those occurring in the real world, changes in attention may also occur as a result of the media's, or the public's, changing *definitions* of certain events or agents or conditions as entailing risk. Even if it is difficult to argue that the media initiate changing definitions of risk, it is clear that they diffuse such changes to audiences previously unaware of them. A story about poverty may—or may not—talk about reduced life expectancy or increased risk of death from various causes among the poor. The risk of death or disability is an aspect of many activities or events. What determines whether that particular aspect will be emphasized by the media or not? Whether associated benefits will be emphasized or not?

Another research question of central interest to this book, then, is variability in the definition of what constitutes a hazard. What

[8]Daniel E. Koshland, Jr., "Interview with a Risk Expert" (editorial), *Science*, vol. 244, no. 4912 (June 30, 1989), p. 1529.

evidence is there of changing definitions over time, and of variations between media? With what other events is it possible to correlate observed changes? To put it a different way, what definitions of risk and risk-taking emerge from a scanning of the mass media? Is riding a bicycle, for example, depicted as a pleasurable activity, an energy saver, a health promoter, a hazard to life and limb—or all of these at various times, and in varying combinations? Are tampons liberating or lethal? Are they, in fact, discussed by the media at all? Is it possible to describe the hazards singled out for media attention in terms of news values, links between news organizations and the social structure, and characteristics of the hazards themselves?

What Information Do the Media Provide about Hazards?

Journalists have been subjected to criticism from various quarters for their reporting on science and technology issues. Some industry representatives, and some government officials as well, see them as more concerned with impact than precision when reporting on such issues as Love Canal, dioxin, and acid rain (cf. Heylin, 1984). Some academic critics, on the other hand, see them as being too deferential to science and scientists, too ready to accept uncritically press releases intended to serve public relations purposes (see, e.g., Nelkin, 1984). Journalists are critical of their own practices in this regard.[9] And still another group of critics complains that journalists pay too much attention to novel and possibly trivial hazards, and far too little to more pervasive but well-known hazards such as smoking.[10]

These comments are for the most part impressionistic. In place of them, this book offers a systematic analysis of a substantial

[9]See, e.g., "Science Sections: Gee Whiz vs. Issues," *The Quill* (November 1984), pp. 56–60.

[10]To which Michael G. Gartner, then president of Des Moines Register and Tribune Co., responds: "New risks do, in fact, receive more publicity than old, known risks. This is because the function of the press is to inform the public so that the public can then make decisions based on that information. The public has been informed about the perils of smoking. The press did its job, the public did its. It is not the function of the press to keep beating the public over the head to quit smoking. The press is not your mother." Quoted in Heylin, *op. cit.*

sample of reporting on risk. In it, we try to answer such questions as the following: Do the media tend to focus on immediate or long-term consequences of hazards? Do they focus on issues or events? How do the media convey the meaning of different types of hazards? For example, are there systematic differences in whether costs or benefits are emphasized for different classes of hazards, or in the precision with which different types of hazard are portrayed? Are there systematic differences in the modes of expressing consequences, all of which may be correct? How detailed is the information communicated about the risks associated with various types of hazards?

Who Gets Blamed?

A third issue with which this book is concerned is that of blame and responsibility. Just as societies vary in their definition of what constitutes a hazard, so too do they vary in the attribution of blame and responsibility for hazard prevention. Given our interest in mass media as both reflectors and shapers of culture, we ask where the media place the locus of control with respect to a given hazard: With the individual? With government? With private industry? With God?

Barton (1969) hypothesized that where there are vested interests in the causes of disasters, mass media content will blame the victim. One might speculate that where there are vested interests in hazards (e.g., cigarettes, alcohol, automobiles) the media will emphasize modes of risk reduction that place the burden of control on the individual rather than on industry regulation. Or, perhaps even more obviously, such hazards may receive no discussion in the media at all. Smith (1978), for example, analyzed articles on smoking in a number of national magazines. In those that accepted cigarette advertising, Smith was "unable to find a single article, in seven years of publication, that would have given readers any clear notion of the nature and extent of the medical and social havoc being wreaked by the cigarette-smoking habit. The records of magazines that refuse cigarette ads, or that do not accept advertising at all, were considerably better." See also Weis and Burke (1986), Kessler (1989), and Warner et al. (1992).

Accuracy and Completeness in Reporting

The final issue with which we concern ourselves in this book is that of the accuracy of reporting on hazards.

Many of the risks of living in contemporary society involve highly complex concepts and highly technical information. Most mass media reporting on them must do so with very little lead time, and most reporters lack both the technical and the statistical training needed to evaluate them on their own. It should therefore come as no surprise if much media coverage of hazards turned out to be less than accurate or complete. Even when they rely on expert sources, reporters may introduce what Fischhoff (1979) has termed a spurious element of precision into a probabilistic process, omitting even those qualifications that their sources are willing to provide.

Many studies of accuracy in reporting exist (e.g., Tankard and Ryan, 1974; Tichenor et al., 1970; Borman, 1978; Broberg, 1973; McCall and Stocking, 1982; Pulford, 1976; Scanlon, Luukko, and Morton, 1978; Meyer, 1988; Shapiro, 1989). All of these are based on some evaluation of a news report, often by the scientist source, and focus on questions such as the following: Are those details which are reported, reported correctly? Are any important details omitted? Has the reporter altered the emphasis in the original source? Have the implications been overgeneralized in the news story?

Summarizing the results of a number of these studies, Dunwoody and Stocking (1985) conclude that science reporting is not more prone to error than general news stories are, when proper controls on the number of error categories are introduced. But information can be accurate without being complete. For example, a story may indicate that tampon users are eighteen times as likely as nonusers to get toxic shock, without specifying the nonuser's odds. It can be argued that with respect to reporting about risks, completeness, including information about elements of uncertainty, is as important as accuracy narrowly defined (cf. Wilson and Crouch, 1987).

Furthermore, Tankard and Ryan (1974) found that "omission of relevant information" about methods and results turned out to be the two most frequent types of error cited by scientists in the reporting of their own work. Although Dunwoody and Stocking (1985) classify this as a "subjective error," it is possible that certain elements of a research report would be regarded as indispensable by most of the scientists involved. Even if no spontaneous agreement exists among scientists, some items of information about research should perhaps become as routine as "who, what, where, and how" are by present conventions.

Related to questions of accuracy and completeness are questions concerning the use of sources for reporting on risk. Some key questions are: What sources are used for reporting on different kinds of hazards? How diverse a group is consulted? How diverse are their institutional affiliations? How much agreement is there among them? Are readers or viewers given any inkling of the relative weight different sources ought to be accorded?

Because of the media's norms of balance and fairness, reporters are likely to seek out, and quote, scientists and policymakers with divergent opinions. The net result of this process may be a spurious image of equally valid opposing positions, an image that serves to confuse, rather than enlighten, the unsophisticated reader. In addition, the presentation of divergent opinions, if there is no "weighting" by either the relative frequency with which they are held or the quality of the evidence on which they are based, may convey an inaccurate, even biased, picture of knowledge in a field.

Variations among Media

One of the problems in analyzing how hazards are reported in the media is that there is no obviously correct benchmark against which to measure either the amount of reporting or its emphases. The strategy we have adopted is to provide an interpretive context by looking at the reporting of hazards in media that one might intuitively expect to differ, both in the kinds of hazards they focus on and in the treatment they provide.

We expected, for example, that hazards emphasized in newspapers for black audiences would differ from those emphasized in newspapers read primarily by white audiences; that health hazards emphasized in *Prevention* magazine would be quite different from those emphasized in the mass media; that hazards depicted in the *Daily News* would differ from those emphasized by the *Wall Street Journal* or the *New York Times*. The inclusion of such contrasting media permits the testing of hypotheses specifying disproportionate media attention to hazards affecting some social groups rather than others, and to mainstream rather than alternative definitions of risk.

Given this interpretive context, we ask how different media vary in their treatment of hazards. For example, to what extent to they cover the same hazards, and to what extent do they specialize? Do newspapers focus on events, whereas newsmagazines pay more attention to issues? How much and what kind of attention is given by different media to varying kinds of hazards? Are there systematic, consistent differences in the completeness with which different media cover the same type of hazard? Finally, do media aimed at different audiences emphasize risks specific to those audiences? Do black newspapers devote more space to sickle cell anemia than newspapers aimed at predominantly white audiences, for example? Do they put a greater emphasis on high blood pressure, which afflicts proportionately more blacks than whites? Do magazines for women emphasize risks specific to women—for example, breast cancer?

RESEARCH DESIGN AND METHODS

The analyses in this book are based on fifteen media monitored for four months in 1984 (September 1 through December 31)[11] and four key media monitored for four weeks (September 4–10, 18–24 and December 11–17, 25–31) in 1960. The media were selected to provide a sampling of national newspaper, newsmagazine, and television coverage as well as purposively planned comparisons with some local media, media aimed at specialized audiences, and media dealing with specialized topics. Our main emphasis, however, was on the national media. As Mazur and Mwaba (1983), among others, have pointed out, "Nearly all national stories are first reported by one or more of a small group of core organizations which we call 'the national media,' including the

---

[11]The *New York Times* and the *Daily News* were monitored only every other week during this period.

New York Times and the *Washington Post,* the three television net-works, *Time* and *Newsweek* magazines, and the two major wire services. . . . These organizations have the resources and connec-tions to cover national (and international) level stories. They can afford specialist reporters who concentrate on science, energy, or environment, and who come to know one another from covering the same events and sometimes sharing accommodations and off hours." Local news outlets largely select their national news from the "menu" of items produced by these organizations. Thus, the public receives a fairly standard news fare, either directly, from the national media, or indirectly, through their recycling by local news sources. Although the proliferation of new news-gathering technologies may lessen the dependence of local television sta-tions on the national networks, these developments did not, at the time of this study, appear to have radically altered the pattern described above.

The specific media monitored in 1984 were the following:

New York Times	ABC News
Daily News	Channel 5 (WNEW)
Wall Street Journal	*Ladies Home Journal*
Amsterdam News	*Ebony*
Newsweek	*Essence*
Time	*New York Magazine*
CBS News	*Prevention*
NBC News	

Of these, only the *Times,* the *Daily News, Time,* and *Newsweek* were monitored in 1960 as well.

During the sampling periods in 1960 and 1984, every story deal-ing with a hazard or group of hazards was selected for analysis. For the most part, the stories featured either a prominent (first two paragraphs) or substantial (one-third of story or more) discus-sion of the hazard; but in a minority of cases, the mention of the hazard occurred more than two paragraphs into the story and occupied less than a third of the space. (However, we did not attempt to catch stories containing only a fleeting hazard ref-erence.)[12]

[12] The actual selection process was much more complex than this description indi-cates. Automobiles are hazards, but we did not, for example, take a story describing a new car model as a story about a hazard. Ordinarily, we required some reference to

After having been selected, each story was assigned to a hazard category (e.g., natural hazards) and given a code number pertaining to a specific hazard within that category (e.g., flood)—either a number already established by Hohenemser and his colleagues, or one added by us. The story was then catalogued by medium, date, and hazard code. The total number of stories selected constitute the universe of all hazard stories appearing in the specified media during our sampling period, and provide the basis for some of the analyses reported later—for example, variations in attention to different kinds of hazards by different media and over time.

From the universe of hazard stories selected and classified in this way (N = 3,828), we chose a smaller number (952 in 1984 and 323 in 1960) for detailed analysis. These stories constitute a random sample of all those appearing in the specified media during the period of our study, but they were not selected in proportion to their actual frequency. Instead, we selected them in such a way as to yield enough stories about a particular hazard in a particular type of medium to permit meaningful analyses. As a rough guide, we aimed at 60 stories per hazard type (e.g., natural disasters) per type of medium (e.g., newspapers) for each sample year, but the total number of hazard stories available did not always permit this. For example, we had only 101 stories altogether about activities involving benefits and costs, and we included all of them for detailed analysis; but this gave us far fewer than 60 per type of medium per year. The analyses reported in the book are based on the unweighted data, but as a check on the generalizability of the findings, we repeated the major analyses using data weighted by the inverse of their probability of selection. With a few exceptions noted in the text, no significant changes emerged

---

an associated risk in order to qualify the story for selection. During the second half of the 1984 monitoring period, we did attempt to select stories about hazards even if they made no mention of risk, because we wanted to try to understand why risks were prominently featured in some stories but not in others. Even during this period, however, we insisted that there be some basis for a discussion of risk in the story. That is, a description of a new car model would not have been selected during this more intensive reading period, either, unless it mentioned some safety feature (or, conversely, some characteristic that made it less safe). For a more detailed description of the selection rules governing the project, see Appendix A.

from these reanalyses. Thus, we believe our findings to apply to the total sample of hazard stories, not simply the subsample selected for detailed analysis. Of course, even the total sample of stories is not representative of the universe of hazard reporting in any way that can be specified precisely, though we aimed at a representative sample of reporting in at least the national media.

For each story selected for detailed examination, we coded a set of media variables—e.g., when and where the story appeared, how long it was, and whether it was accompanied by graphics of any kind. (For an example of a coding form, see Appendix B.) For each, we also coded a set of variables pertaining to the main hazard dealt with in the story. These variables included the factual details in the story; the locus of blame or responsibility; the sources quoted; the research cited; the groups noted as being at risk; the proportion of the story devoted to risks and to benefits, and so on. Most of these variables were identical for all hazards, but there was some variation between coding forms. We did not, for example, ask about the "benefits" of natural hazards.

Each story was coded by one of six coders, and then edited by another coder or one of the two co-authors. For most of the substantive variables, editing involved double coding, with disagreements resolved by discussions between coder and editor. On an earlier project involving similar coding decisions and many of the same coders, the average coefficient of agreement (kappa) after training was .517, with a range from .029 to .783. Values of kappa from .41–.60 are considered moderate (Landis and Koch, 1977). After the data had been entered for computer processing, they were further checked for logical inconsistencies and out-of-range codes.

ORGANIZATION OF THE BOOK

The book has been organized around the key issues outlined earlier in this chapter. To begin with, Chapter 2 presents a descriptive account of the way some specific hazards have been reported; it offers, as it were, a natural history of hazard reporting, although limited to hazards of a particularly dramatic kind. Issues of hazard definition are discussed in Chapters 3 and 4; issues of presentation, in Chapter 5. Chapter 6 deals with the assigning of blame and responsibility for hazards or their prevention. Chapter 7 examines the role of sources, and Chapter 8 analyzes the accuracy of hazard reporting. Variations among media are discussed in each of these chapters. Chapter 9 summarizes the findings and presents our conclusions. Appendix A discusses our selection and coding procedures in greater detail than has been possible in this chapter, and Appendix B presents illustrations of the coding forms we used for the content analysis.

2 / The Natural History of Hazard Reporting

The function of the news media is to report on events, not to anticipate them and not, with rare exceptions, to investigate the reasons for their occurrence. Although Tuchman (1978), Altheide (1976, 1985), and other authors (e.g., Epstein, 1973) of now classic works contend that the media construct reality instead of merely reflecting it, what they mean by this is that the media select, emphasize, and arrange. They do not question the fact that, ordinarily, the news media react to events rather than initiating coverage of an issue.

To say this is not to disparage or criticize the performance of journalists, but simply to acknowledge the role they play in contemporary United States society. Their job is to give the news after it has happened. Even a scoop, every journalist's dream, only anticipates the occurrence of an event—or, more likely, other journalists' coverage of an event—by a little while. Just as "the press is not your mother," so it is not a prognosticator of events likely to take place, if at all, in the distant future. Only if someone who is "news," or who speaks on a newsworthy occasion, engages in such rites of prediction will the media bother to report them.

tion, it turned out to be, as Perrow (1986:350, 354–56) put it, "only an accident . . . that in Institute the tank held aldicarb oxime rather than the more toxic MIC, also made there, and that the aldicarb tank was not full, and that the wind was not just right and so on. . . . Risky systems are full of failures. Inevitably, though less frequently, these failures will interact in unexpected ways, defeat the safety devices and bring down the system. . . . But even this might not produce a catastrophe unless there is also a rare combination of weather and wind conditions, a time and a place where people are present in large numbers, and no warning."

As of December 3, 1985, the lawsuits against Union Carbide as a result of the Bhopal accident were still unresolved, and a number of those hospitalized in Institute, West Virginia, had filed suit as well. On August 5, 1986, the *Times* reported that, after months of negotiations, a civil suit against Union Carbide would be filed in India, the case having been dismissed by a U.S. federal judge as inappropriately filed in the United States. The case had not yet been settled as of November 19, 1987, almost three years after the accident. On December 2, 1987, the *Times* reported that the government of India had filed criminal charges against Union Carbide, Warren M. Anderson, the chairman who resigned after the accident, and eight Indians in the deaths of "at least 2800 people" (8,000, according to Dan Kurzman, a former correspondent for the *Washington Post,* in *A Killing Wind*).

Thus, some three years after the initial accident, the risk issues posed by the event were essentially unresolved. The specific damage claims of those who had been injured or whose relatives had died had not yet been settled; responsibility for the accident had not been established; and the more general risk issues raised by the event—namely, the risks to populations posed by chemical plants here and abroad, and whether and how those risks might be reduced—were only beginning to be investigated. The last issue was addressed by some reporters in the context of the accident at Institute, West Virginia, but then the story again dropped from sight.

Only in February 1989 was the lawsuit finally settled by an order of the Indian Supreme Court, which ordered Union Carbide to pay India $470 million in damages. As part of the settlement, the Court ordered the dismissal of all criminal charges and other civil suits in India against Union Carbide and its chairman at the time of the accident, Warren M. Anderson (*New York Times*, Feb. 16, 1989, p. 1). Even then, many details of how the money would be disbursed to victims remained unresolved, and no payments had yet been made as of October 1991. In fact, by then the issue of a settlement had once again been clouded by the Court's demand that criminal proceedings against those responsible for the leak be reinstituted.

It became clear long after the accident that some of the initial U.S. reporting on the risks of MIC had been in error. Specifically, serious injuries appeared to be much more frequent and longer-lasting than originally reported, and hydrogen cyanide appeared to have been involved in some of these effects. Reporters may be, as Rothman and the Lichters (1986) claim, more liberal than the population in general, but they are nevertheless source-dependent. In the case of the accident at Bhopal, their necessary reliance on U.S. industry sources for much of the information about MIC and its production seems to have resulted in initial underestimates of the severity and extent of injuries.[3] Although some media reported these new developments as they became known, the likelihood is that they were correctly perceived by only a small fraction of those who had followed the original reports. Both of these characteristics (i.e., the waning of media attention before long-term issues have been resolved, and the initial reporting of some erroneous details) characterize reporting about many hazards, with consequences we consider later.

BABY FAE

On October 26, 1984, a 12-day-old infant, Baby Fae, who was suffering from a heart defect that, if untreated, would result in death within days or weeks, underwent the world's first baboon-to-baby heart transplant at Loma Linda Medical Center in Califor-

---

[3] In the case of Chernobyl, the deliberate withholding of information by the USSR combined with a variety of prejudgments to produce large *overestimates* of the disaster's immediate effects. The first headlines spoke of thousands of deaths, though these estimates were revised downward within the next few days. Gale (1987) reported that 31 people died in the immediate aftermath of the radiation release—2 initially and 29 within two months. Predictions of long-term fatalities attributable to Chernobyl vary widely, from 5,000 to 40,000.

tion" [May 14, 1990]). Nor was there any outpouring of aid comparable to that in 1984.

SUMMARY AND CONCLUSION

We began this chapter by saying that the media are reactive, ordinarily reporting on hazards that have already occurred instead of anticipating them. But this does not mean that they allocate their attention in proportion to the *risks* associated with these hazards.

An early study, by Funkhouser (1973), already indicated this quite clearly. Examining the attention devoted by the media (as indexed by the number of articles in *Time, Newsweek,* and *U.S. News and World Report*) to various domestic and international issues, as well as external indicators of their severity, he found at best a modest relationship between the two. Funkhouser also pointed out the same two tendencies we have noted in this chapter (p. 73, emphasis supplied):

> Coverage of issues based on *newsworthy* events—the war, urban riots, student unrest, and crime—seemed to involve a sort of "adaptation" of the media to the stream of events, by which a pattern of events ceased to be "news" after a while. The coverage of all these issues declined before the events themselves reached their peak. . . . Coverage of issues based on *non*-newsworthy events . . . seemed to be primarily a function of "artificial news."

Furthermore, news organizations do not cover risk in the abstract: they cover "newsworthy events" (as defined by their own norms and guild values) that happen to entail risks to life and health. Thus, their reporting on risk is governed by the same decision rules as the reporting of other news. They are constrained by a range of factors: knowledge and availability of sources, schedules, deadlines, skills and knowledge of their staffs, and, for television, the number of camera crews and the availability of film.

But the fact that reporting about hazards and risks is generally not defined as such has certain consequences. News stories about hazards ordinarily do not provide enough information to permit rational decisions. They alert us to danger. They perform a "surveillance" function, as Lasswell long ago aptly put it, but for the most part they do not accurately inform us about either the dimensions of the danger or the risks of alternatives. That is not their intent.[9] Even when the intent is to provide information useful for reducing risks, the information is often inadequate and sometimes inaccurate (cf. Chapter 8, on reporting accuracy). The result is that emotion, not reason, is likely to govern our response to those hazards for which we depend on the media for information. The media make the most of mayhem, but this brief focusing of attention on crisis situations may well be dysfunctional for rational public attitudes and behavior.

---

[9]Post et al. (1986:26) state this explicitly in relation to reporting on radon in the Lehigh Valley in Pennsylvania: "[T]he local newspapers played a vital role in alerting readers in the Lehigh Valley about the radon problem. However, . . . they did not appear to bring a clear understanding of its complexities to readers."

words, they presented a biased impression of risk, if by bias we mean a systematically distorted representation of the actuarial risks involved.

But both of these are instances of one specific hazard, namely, violent crime. Because we were interested in analyzing the issue of bias more generally, we were forced to take a somewhat indirect approach. In this chapter, we consider three questions, all of them bearing on the more general issue of which hazards the media feature, and which they ignore. The first asks for which hazards the media always report on associated harms (that is, injury, illness, property damage, or death), for which they do so only sometimes, and for which types of hazards they never include a discussion of harm.

The second question examines the relation between the kinds of hazards attended to by the media and their importance as causes of death. The question of bias raised by this analysis asks whether certain kinds of hazards are underreported or overreported in relation to the number of deaths they cause in the United States. In this analysis, we look at all the deaths caused by a particular category of hazard, ignoring the characteristics of its victims. The third question posed in this chapter asks *whose risks* are emphasized by the media, again across a variety of hazards. In the chapter that follows, we pursue the analysis of which risks are attended to by the media, and which are ignored, by looking at the effect of geographic location on this process.

We begin the chapter with certain descriptive statistics, which summarize variations in the distribution of hazard reporting between media and over time, and conclude it by asking how public perceptions of risk are affected by media coverage.

VARIATIONS IN HAZARD REPORTING OVER TIME AND BETWEEN MEDIA

The distribution of news stories, by hazard category and year, is shown in Table 3.1. This table is based on all the stories monitored in both years, not merely those selected for detailed analysis. As is apparent from Table 3.1, most of the hazard stories came from media monitored in 1984—not because there were more such stories then, but because we monitored many more media, and for

TABLE 3.1 / Distribution of News Stories among Hazard Categories 1960 and 1984

	1960		1984	
Hazard Category	(%)	(N)	(%)	(N)
Natural hazards	12.8	(96)	11.2	(344)
Activities with benefits and costs	2.9	(22)	3.3	(101)
Energy hazards	62.7	(470)	32.8	(1,010)
Materials hazards	6.5	(49)	27.7	(854)
Complex technologies	2.3	(17)	12.0	(370)
Illnesses	8.8	(66)	8.1	(250)
Miscellaneous other hazards	4.0	(30)	4.8	(149)
TOTAL	100.0	(750)	99.9	(3,078)

a longer period of time. When we looked at the number of stories controlling for these two factors, the 1960 and 1984 total figures were identical. Thus, there does not appear to have been any more attention to hazards—at least on the part of the *News*, the *Times, Time,* and *Newsweek,* which are the four media analyzed in both time periods—in 1984 than there had been in 1960.

The most striking difference between the 1960 and 1984 distributions involves changes in the frequency with which energy hazards were reported. By 1984, the percentage of energy hazard stories, which made up the overwhelming majority of hazard stories in 1960, had been cut in half, and the proportion of stories about materials hazards and complex technologies had greatly increased. There was virtually no change in the relative frequencies with which other hazards were reported.

The findings hold true when we look at the number of different hazards (instead of the number of stories)[3] reported on in both years; and they hold, as well, when we look only at stories in the four media we monitored in both years.

Looking at changes in the coverage of specific hazards, we find

[3]Looking at the number of different hazards controls for the possible confounding effect of having a very large number of stories associated with one or two specific hazards (e.g., the release of methyl isocyanate in Bhopal, which accounted for 173 stories in our 1984 sample).

TABLE 3.2 / Distribution of News Stories among Hazard Categories (All News Stories, 1984 Only)

Hazard Category	Newspapers (%)	Weeklies (%)	Television (%)	Monthlies (%)
Natural hazards	9.0	15.2	14.2	0.0
Activities and benefits and costs	3.7	2.5	2.5	13.6
Energy hazards	33.4	21.5	34.0	9.1
Materials hazards	29.3	29.7	25.0	27.3
Complex technologies	10.4	14.6	14.3	4.5
Illnesses	7.8	12.7	7.3	40.9
Miscellaneous other hazards	6.2	3.8	2.8	4.5
(N)	(1,762)	(158)	(1,136)	(22)

that stories about the space shuttle and about nuclear war were much more numerous in 1984 than they had been in 1960, though neither type of story mentioned the associated risks. Organ transplants gave rise to 4 stories in 1960 compared with 259 in 1984, most of the latter accounted for by the implantation of the world's second artificial heart. AIDS, unknown in 1960, was discussed in 48 stories in 1984. Materials hazards of all kinds were more often in the news in 1984 than they had been in 1960, with stories about nuclear reactors, toxic waste, MIC, and other chemicals especially numerous. One notable exception was that of nuclear tests, which generated 10 stories in 1960, compared with only 4 in 1984.

The media in our sample differ in the attention they give to different hazards. Even in 1960, the newsweeklies carried relatively fewer stories about energy hazards than the dailies did, and relatively more stories about complex technologies and illness. But differences among media can be seen more clearly in Table 3.2, which presents distributions separately for newspapers (including the *Amsterdam News*), newsweeklies, monthlies, and television newscasts (including Channel 5 WNEW) for 1984 only. Except for *Prevention*, the monthly magazines we looked at (*Ebony, Essence, Ladies' Home Journal*)—carried virtually no stories about hazards. *Prevention*, by definition, carried virtually nothing else, and not unexpectedly featured a relatively greater number of stories about illness.

Differences among the remaining media are not very large.

Newspapers featured fewer stories about natural hazards than either television or the newsweeklies. The weeklies, as was true in 1960, carried fewer stories about energy hazards and more about illness than either newspapers or television newscasts did. In fact, *Time's* distribution of hazard stories was similar to that of the newspapers; it was *Newsweek* which was the real maverick in 1984.

The dramatic difference, however, is not between different media at one point in time, but between the two time periods in our sample. And this difference—the huge shift from concern over energy hazards, which pose immediate risks to their victims, to concern over materials hazards, especially contamination of the environment by chemical pollutants that do much of their damage over the long run—does represent a long-term societal trend. The big news about hazards in the eighties was news about environmental hazards assumed to be capable of causing illness and death in the future, though, as we shall see in Chapter 5, most of the stories about these hazards contain very little information about the risks involved.

MEDIA DEFINITIONS OF RISK

In order to get at media definitions of risk, we look next at the type of coverage given by the media to different hazards. The discussion in this section is based not on the total number of hazard stories we observed in the media ("the universe") but on the smaller subset selected for detailed analysis.

By "type of coverage," in this context, we mean something very specific: Did the media story (1) deal with risk-related *issues,* (2) treat the hazard as a self-contained *event,* or (3) *fail to mention* any associated risk at all?[4] The first type of story includes reports of issues and/or data related to a hazard or a hazardous condition or event (e.g., a discussion of causes, prevention, treatment, or ethical issues). The second consists of reports of self-contained

---

[4]Sandman et al. (1987) noted that an environmental hazards story can go in one of four directions: a damage story (who died, who was injured?); a risk story (what's going to happen, how much damage will there be, how serious is the risk?); a blame story; or a clean-up story (what are they going to do about it?). Sandman's last three categories are subsumed in our issue category.

occurrences of a hazard (e.g, a fire, someone's illness, a car crash, a release of toxic gas). Such a story, which Sandman et al. (1987) refer to as a "damage" story, reports on who died, who was injured, or what kind of property damage occurred, but on no other issues or data. We called this an "event-only" story. The final type of story reports on an event or condition potentially treated as risky (e.g., mountain climbing), but with no specific mention of risk,[5] or stories about an event or condition potentially risky, but not a risk in this particular case (e.g., a specific power failure that might have caused death or injury but did not, or a near-miss of an airplane collision).

This classification scheme immediately tells us something about how the media define risk. First, if a news story about a hazard carries no information about associated harms, then that hazard is not defined as risky by the media. For example, as we will see below, none of the stories about the space shuttle in our sample mentioned the possibility of harm to the crew. The shuttle was not defined by the media as entailing risk in 1984, prior to the *Challenger* explosion.[6]

Second, if a news story was classified by us as an event-only story, it carried information about harms associated with a specific incident of a hazard (a car crash, a fire), but the *probability* of harm from that hazard was implicit, and had to be inferred by the viewer or reader.

What proportion of hazard stories fell into these two categories, and what kinds of hazards were likely to be defined by the media as isolated events or as not entailing risk at all?

In 1960, event-only stories made up almost half the total number of those selected for analysis. By 1984, that proportion had dropped to 31.3 percent. In both years, however, activities involving benefits and costs and, to a lesser extent, natural hazards, were most likely to be treated as event-only or, in Sandman's term, "damage" stories.

---

[5]In general, we use "risk" to refer to the *probability* of harm. But when, in this chapter, we refer to an absence of information about risk, we mean that there was no mention of harm at all, not simply an absence of probability information.

[6]However, while it is easy enough to distinguish event-only from issue stories, it is much more difficult to identify hazard stories in which there is no mention of risk at all, because such identification *presupposes prior knowledge of what constitutes a hazard.* Since this is precisely what we often lack, it is likely that some unknown number of stories failing to mention associated risks were not recognized by us as hazard stories at all.

TABLE 3.3 / Risk Definitions for Different Hazard Categories, by Year (Analysis Subsample)

Hazard Category	Presents Risk-Related Issues		Event-Only Story		No Mention of Risk/ Harm[a]	
	1960 (%)	1984 (%)	1960 (%)	1984 (%)	1960 (%)	1984 (%)
Natural hazards	42.4	59.6	56.1	40.4	1.5	—
Activities with benefits and costs	19.0	47.8	81.0	47.8	—	4.4
Energy hazards	45.4	55.4	50.0	39.2	4.6	5.4
Materials hazards	51.4	77.8	25.5	18.7	23.4	3.5
Complex technologies	75.0	67.6	12.5	27.6	12.5	4.8
Illnesses	61.5	73.3	36.9	25.3	1.5	1.3
TOTAL %	48.6	65.5	45.2	31.3	6.2	3.2
(N)	(157)	(624)	(146)	(298)	(20)	(30)
	$\chi^2 = 41.42;$		$\chi^2 = 28.23;$			
	$df = 5;$		$df = 5;$			
	$p < .01$		$p < .01$			

[a] 1960 and 1984 stories about nuclear war, which rarely mentioned risk, and 1984 stories about the space shuttle, which never mentioned risk, have been excluded from this tabulation because they were not part of the analysis sample. Cell sizes are too small to permit a reliable calculation of chi-square.

About 6 percent of hazard stories selected for detailed analysis in 1960, and 3 percent in 1984, failed to mention harms altogether. Those about materials hazards in 1960, especially stories about nuclear reactors and nuclear tests, were especially likely to fail to mention associated harms. In 1984, there were few differences in this regard among hazard categories. With the exception of natural hazards (where no stories failed to mention associated harms), between 1 percent and 5 percent of stories involving each type of hazard made no mention of the associated harms (see Table 3.3).

This discussion must be qualified by noting that *we deleted from the detailed analysis all 1984 space shuttle stories, because none of them mentioned harm, and most 1960 and 1984 stories about nuclear war, because these also failed to mention harm.*[7] Thus, the two most numerous categories of hazard stories that failed to mention associated

[7] The dearth of network coverage of nuclear war issues is documented as well by Rubin and Cummings (1989), who analyze such coverage between 1982 and 1986.

harms were stories about nuclear war and stories about the space shuttle, but since both of these categories were deliberately excluded from the detailed analysis, they do not appear at all in the figures cited above.

In 1984, the percentage of all stories discussing risk factors or issues was substantially higher than it had been in 1960—65.5 percent, compared with 48.6 percent.[8] Stories involving benefit-and-cost activities were again less likely than the average story to discuss such factors, and illness (73.3 percent) and materials hazards (77.8 percent) were especially likely to do so. But while issue stories were the only ones with the potential for defining risk explicitly, very few such stories actually did so (see Chapter 5).[9]

The analysis in this section reinforces what has been said about the reactivity of the media in Chapter 2. Particularly striking in this regard, during our sampling period, was the media's failure to define as a hazard either nuclear war or the space shuttle, even though news stories about both of these abounded, especially in 1984.

MEDIA HAZARDS AS CAUSES OF DEATH

In this section, we compare the frequency with which certain hazards are featured in the media with the number of annual deaths they cause in the U.S., as one plausible surrogate for an objective universe of hazards. One earlier study, by Combs and Slovic (1979), had looked at all causes of death reported in two small local newspapers over a period of a year and found very low Pearson correlations (.19 and .21, respectively) between the number of deaths caused annually by forty-one hazards (e.g., by earthquakes, as reported in statistical sources) and the attention they received in the press, as measured by the number of stories appearing in the two newspapers. (However, the rank order correlation between the two was substantially higher: .62 for one newspaper and .66 for the other.)

---

[8]Others have commented on the increasing tendency for the media to report on issues rather than events only as "the new long journalism." See, for example, Barnhurst (1991), Barnhurst and Nerone (1991), and Mutz (1992).

[9]Sandman and his colleagues (1987) reported that the absence of risk information in newspaper stories that were ostensibly about environmental risk was one of the most striking findings of their study. They found, for example, that only 30 percent of the paragraphs they analyzed contained any information about risk.

Our study provided an opportunity to look at the relation between hazards as causes of death and as topics of news stories for a much wider array of both media and hazards, and to replicate the analysis for two separate years. The stories did not necessarily mention any associated deaths, but the hazards were all potential causes of either injury or death. We correlated death rates for causes of death reported in the *Statistical Abstract of the United States* for 1988 with the corresponding categories in our media sample,[10] using for this purpose the universe of hazard stories (N = 3,078 in 1984 and 750 in 1960). For some of these, of course, we did not find any stories in the media during our period of observation—for example, syphilis. There were fifteen such categories (out of forty-one) in 1984 and twenty-three (out of forty-four) in 1960. For these, a zero was correlated with the death rate. The results of this analysis are shown in Table 3.4.

As can be seen from Table 3.4, the correlations between number of stories and number of deaths, whether computed by a Pearson *r* or a rank-order coefficient, are very small. Because it seemed to us that the explanation for this might lie in the existence of a number of outliers—for example, in 1984, accidental poisoning, largely comprised of stories about methyl isocyanate, and complications due to medical procedures, largely comprised of stories about an artificial heart implant and about Baby Fae—we repeated the analysis excluding these outliers.[11] Although the correlations increased somewhat, they were still not significantly different from zero.[12]

Interestingly enough, however, the correlation between the

[10] Seven categories listed as causes of death in the *Statistical Abstract* were excluded from the analysis: suicides and homicides, for which we did not keep a precise count of stories; and "other" industrial accidents, "all other accidents," "ill-defined symptoms and conditions," "other infective and parasitic diseases," and "all other causes," because of ambiguities in matching these to our coding categories.

[11] They are outliers because in 1984 they resulted in many news stories, although ordinarily they cause few deaths. Of course, the fact that they are out of the ordinary is one reason they are news!

[12] There are several possible reasons for the difference between Combs and Slovic's (1979) findings and our own. In the first place, Combs and Slovic included four natural hazards among their forty-one causes; we included none because none were included in the *Statistical Abstract* listing. Second, they double- (and sometimes even triple-) counted both deaths and stories. For example, breast cancer, stomach cancer, and lung cancer are listed separately by them, but there is also an "all cancer" category as well as an "all disease" category; and while some accidents are enumerated separately, there is also an "all accidents" category.

TABLE 3.4 / Correlation Between Number of Stories and Death Rates for Selected Causes of Death, 1960 and 1984[a]

Diseases	1960 Number of Stories	1960 Death Rate	1984 Number of Stories	1984 Death Rate
Diseases of the heart	13	369.0	26	323.5
Hypertension	0	7.1	2	3.3
Cerebrovascular diseases	1	108.0	4	65.3
Atherosclerosis	3	20.0	1	10.3
Other cardiovascular diseases	0	11.0	0	9.2
Malignancies	11	149.2	39	191.8
Chronic obstructive pulmonary and allied conditions (besides emphysema, etc.)	0	9.9	0	29.2
Bronchitis, chronic and unspecified	0	1.8	0	1.5
Acute bronchitis and bronchiolitis	0	0.7	0	0.2
Emphysema	0	5.2	1	5.6
Asthma	2	3.0	0	1.5
Pneumonia	0	32.9	0	24.4
Influenza	1	4.4	8	0.5
Diabetes mellitus	0	16.7	2	15.1
Chronic liver disease and cirrhosis	0	11.3	0	11.6
Conditions originating in perinatal period (early infancy)	0	37.4	1	8.0
Nephritis, nephrotic syndrome and nephrosis and infections of kidney	1	11.9	2	9.4
Congenital anomalies	4	12.2	7	5.5
Septicemia	0	1.1	0	6.4
Ulcer of stomach and duodenum	0	6.3	0	2.8
Benign neoplasm	0	2.7	0	2.7
Hernia of abdominal cavity and intestinal obstruction	0	5.1	0	2.2
Anemias (including sickle-cell anemia)	0	1.9	3	1.5
Cholelithiasis and other disorders of gall bladder	0	2.6	0	1.3

TABLE 3.4 / (*continued*)

Diseases	1960 Number of Stories	1960 Death Rate	1984 Number of Stories	1984 Death Rate
Nutritional deficiencies	1	4.3	2	0.9
Tuberculosis	4	6.1	0	0.7
Meningitis	0	1.3	0	0.5
Hyperplasia of prostate	0	2.5	0	0.2
Viral hepatitis	3	0.5	4	0.4
Syphilis	0	1.6	N/A	—
Accidents and Adverse Effects				
Motor vehicle accidents	108	21.3	158	19.6
Other road vehicle accidents	0	0.1	2	N/A
Water transport accidents	34	0.8	24	0.5
Air and space transport accidents	118	0.8	120	0.5
Railway accidents	20	0.6	67	0.2
Accidental falls	12	10.6	17	5.0
Accidental drowning	5	2.9	5	1.9
Accidents caused by fire	97	4.3	161	2.1
Accidents caused by firearms	19	1.3	35	0.7
Accidents caused by electrical current	1	0.6	4	0.4
Accidents caused by explosive material	22	N/A	66	N/A
Accidents caused by hot substance/corrosive liquid	0	0.2	0	N/A
Accidents caused by cutting/piercing instrument	0	N/A	1	N/A
Accidental poisoning	0	1.6	199	2.1
Complications due to medical procedure	16	0.6	317	1.1
Inhalation and ingestion of objects	0	1.3	1	1.5
Spearman r:	.03, $N = 44$, $p = .83$		$-.05$, $N = 41$, $p = .74$	
Pearson r:	.001, $N = 44$, $p = .99$		$-.08$, $N = 41$, $p = .93$	

[a]Death rates are unadjusted for age. Source: *Statistical Abstract of the United States, 1988*, Tables 117 and 123. For 1960 death rates for accidents, *Statistical Abstract of the United States, 1986*, Table 120. Causes of death that do not appear in the *Statistical Abstract* are indicated by "N/A."

TABLE 3.5 / Whose Risks Do the Media Report?[a]

Social Category	1960 (%)	1984 (%)
Gender		
Men	80.0	34.5
Women	20.0	41.4
Both equally	0.0	24.1
(N)	(5)	(29)
Race		
White	0.0	23.1
Black	100.0	61.5
Other	0.0	7.7
No difference	0.0	7.7
(N)	(1)	(13)
Age		
Children	75.0	35.6
Young adults	0.0	6.9
Middle-aged adults	0.0	2.0
Older adults	12.5	15.8
Other	0.0	39.6
No difference	12.5	0.0
(N)	(8)	(101)
Class		
Middle-class	0.0	2.6
Working-class	0.0	2.6
Poor	0.0	84.2
Other	0.0	2.6
No difference	100.0	7.9
(N)	(1)	(38)

[a]Based on stories in which one or more social or demographic categories were explicitly mentioned. The number of 1960 stories is too small to permit the calculation of chi-squares.

efits and costs were also more likely than the average story to contain such references.

But where they existed, these references do not support the hypothesis of differential media attention to the risks of the more affluent and powerful. True, in 1960, 4 of the 5 stories that mentioned gender mentioned men as being at risk (see Table 3.5). But in 1984, 41.4 percent of the 29 stories mentioning gender were concerned with hazards affecting primarily women, and another 24.1 percent with hazards affecting both women and men. The one story in 1960 that mentioned race made reference to the risk of blacks; in 1984, 61.5 percent of the 13 stories referring to race specifically mentioned blacks as being at risk. And 84.2 percent of the 38 stories mentioning class dealt with the hazards of poor people.

We also created an index on which a story was scored 1 if it explicitly referred to blacks, women, the elderly, or the poor; and 0 if it referred to none of these. We expected stories dealing with any of these groups to be shorter, on average, than stories making no reference to them. In fact, however, they were longer. In 1960, only three stories mentioned one of these groups. They were longer than other stories, though not significantly so. In 1984, both print ($N = 44$) and television ($N = 18$) stories dealing with disadvantaged groups were significantly longer than other stories.[14] There was no difference so far as the prominence of the stories was concerned.

But while our hypothesis concerning the space devoted to those stories that do mention certain status categories was not supported, we interpret the small number of stories dealing explicitly with the risks of these social categories as an indicator of mass media neglect.[15] Stories about illness, for example, almost never make reference to differential incidence by socioeconomic status, even though many diseases take a far higher toll of lower-status groups. One of the few stories paying explicit attention to such differences is one in the *Times* (January 13, 1989, p. 1). Headlined "Racial Differences Found in Kind of Medical Care Americans Get," it reports on a detailed study of differential application of certain medical procedures by race, even when other variables, such as income, are controlled.

---

[14] Turk et al. (1989:113) report a similar finding: "Hispanic stories and photos in the *Journal* and *Express* are generally longer, and get bigger headlines and more prominent placement. . . ."

[15] This approach is similar to one adopted by Raymond (1985), who carried out a quantitative analysis of the coverage of occupational health issues in several mainstream and advocacy publications between 1970 and 1982. Occupational hazards are a significant source of morbidity and mortality in developed countries. None of the media examined devoted more than 3 percent of their news space to the topic, but the mainstream publications devoted less space to problems of occupational health than the advocacy journals did. Raymond interprets this as an indication of mass media neglect. The difficulty with this analysis, as we have already noted, is that there is no readily available yardstick by which to measure how much coverage would have been enough.

It is possible that reporting about minorities suffers from the same biases as coverage of underdeveloped countries is alleged to do (Rosenblum, 1981; see Chapter 4). For example, the study by Turk (1989) found that coverage of Hispanic-Americans in two southwestern newspapers had improved in the eighties, and that Hispanics and Hispanic issues were present in the newspaper news space in proportion to their presence in the population. Nevertheless, like other studies, this one found that Hispanic news tended to focus on Hispanics as "'problem people,' causing or beset by problems" more often than this was true of Anglos.[16] Clearly, presenting differential risks accurately without at the same time reinforcing negative stereotypes is not an easy assignment.

OTHER FACTORS INFLUENCING COVERAGE

In this section, we ask what factors, aside from social status, influence the amount of coverage a hazard story receives, once it has been selected for coverage. Ideally, we would like to know what determines selection, but lacking an independent source of information about the distribution of hazards, we substitute an analysis based on the media reports themselves. We examined two factors potentially influencing coverage: the extent of harm associated with a specific instance of a hazard; and whether or not the hazard is a new one. (A third potential factor—the region of the world in which the hazard occurred—is examined in Chapter 4.)

We begin by looking at associated harm, defining this in terms of the number of actual or potential deaths and injuries mentioned in connection with the specific hazard episode.[17] We then examine the effect of the newness of the particular hazard involved. Other

[16] In the late eighties, the Gannett news organization, reflecting a concern with the negative tenor of news about minorities, implemented an "affirmative action" policy for news content: "Reporters and photographers [were] strongly encouraged to interview and take pictures of members of minority groups for all kinds of stories, not just those about racial issues, and to find stories and pictures that present minorities in a positive light. . . . Gannett executives describe their 'mainstreaming' policy as an effort to . . . make minority groups more visible in the chain's news pages, and to get away from what one official calls 'the insidious stereotyping that tends to take place by white male managers' " (Nickerson, 1989:16).

[17] Hohenemser and his colleagues (1983) define other important descriptive dimensions of risk, such as spatial extent and number of generations affected, but these were

things being equal, we assumed new hazards would get more coverage than old.

The Effect of Associated Harm on Amount of Coverage

We hypothesized that hazard stories mentioning associated deaths or injuries would be longer than those that failed to mention such risks, and would be featured more prominently. By "prominently" we mean being featured on the front page, or on the front page of another section of a newspaper; being reported with an interview or film on television; or being featured as the cover story of a magazine.

As we expected, hazard stories mentioning deaths were indeed more prominent than other kinds of hazard stories. In 1960 the differences were very small and not statistically significant. But in 1984, 36.4 percent of stories mentioning deaths were prominently featured, compared with 26 percent of those that did not ($X^2 = 10.05$; $p = .0015$). However, mention of injuries made no significant difference in prominence either in 1960 or in 1984.

Both in 1960 and in 1984 hazard stories that mentioned death or injury were longer than those stories that did not. In 1960 the mean length of stories mentioning deaths was 8.4 column inches, compared with 6.7 column inches for those that did not. For those mentioning injury, the figures were 9.0 vs. 7.4. (Both sets of figures are significant at better than the .05 level.) For 1984, the means were 16.1 vs. 11.8 column inches and 28.7 vs. 20.5 lines of television scripts for deaths; for injuries, the comparable figures were 16.35 vs. 12.63 column inches and 26.87 vs. 24.20 lines. The figures for print are statistically significant; for television they are not.

Furthermore, when a story mentions deaths or injuries, there are moderate correlations, both in print and on television, between the number of deaths or injuries reported and the amount of space or time given to the story.[18] For print, the correlations in 1984 were .24 for number of deaths and .27 for number of injuries;

---

almost never mentioned in the stories we examined (see Chapter 5). Nor was annual mortality, which would be a useful corrective to fatality figures associated with a given incident.

[18] Deaths and injuries were coded on a logarithmic scale, as follows: 1–10, 11–100, 101–1,000, 1,000–10,000, etc.

for television, the correlations were .32 for number of deaths and .25 for number of injuries. All but the last of these coefficients are significant at well beyond the .01 level; for the last correlation, based on 54 cases, $p = .03$.

The Effect of Newness of the Hazard

Only 2.5 percent of the hazard stories in 1960, and 4.6 percent in 1984, labeled the hazard as a new one. In 1984, stories about hazards that were called new were longer, on average, than those that were not (22.3 vs. 13.7 column inches; $t = 3.27$, $p < .01$; 30.1 television lines vs. 24.1 lines, *ns*); they also tended to be featured prominently more often (43.2 percent vs. 30.9 percent; *ns*). Because of the small number of stories referring to new hazards in 1960, we did not carry out the analysis for that year.

We also, however, independently classified the main hazard of all 1984 stories as new or not, regardless of the journalist's classification.[19] Stories about hazards we classified as new were longer than those about other hazards, but not significantly so, and they were also more likely to be prominently featured.

But while most news stories are not about "new" hazards, they are about hazards occurring "now." In 1984, 75.8 percent of energy and natural hazards reported had occurred either "now" or within a "few days" of now. In the case of materials hazards, for which we used a slightly different coding scheme, 62.2 percent of stories in 1984 and 83.4 percent in 1960 referred to events occurring either in the present or in the near future. This well-known bias in favor of immediacy may combine with other biases—for example, toward the exciting and the dramatic—to limit coverage of chronic hazards such as illness, which ordinarily have no clear time frame. It may also be a factor limiting coverage of

---

[19]The following hazards were classified by us as new, meaning they had surfaced in the media within a year or two of our study: AIDS; gene splicing; gene therapy; organ transplants (artificial; baboon); video display terminals; chelation therapy; euthanasia; medical devices (a shock-wave device for dissolving kidney stones); coronary angioplasty; suction lipectomy; heart surgery (installation of a heart pump); coronary imaging; chorionic villus sampling.

Our classification was more liberal than that of the journalists. We classified 117 stories as dealing with new hazards; they referred to new hazards in only 44. Apart from this, agreement was reasonably good; phi between the two distributions was .466.

poverty and hazardous working conditions, unless some dramatic happening makes these "news."

BIASED COVERAGE AND THE PERCEPTION OF RISK

We have seen that media coverage of hazards is biased, as evaluated against the number of deaths they cause annually. The media overemphasize dramatic accidents causing multiple fatalities, and underreport illnesses that claim the vast proportion of lives. Other biases appear to be present as well—for example, new hazards are likely to receive disproportionate emphasis, and hazards specific to certain groups may be underreported or overreported. These biases are what journalists and those who study them ordinarily refer to as news values.

The question we raise in this section is: What difference do these biases, to the extent that they exist, make in public perceptions of various risks? In order to answer it, we ideally need studies in which media reports of risk are at variance with reality. This section summarizes some studies bearing on this question, even though not all of them have been defined as dealing with risk (see also Johnson and Covello, 1987:179).

Slovic, Fischhoff, and Lichtenstein (1979), in the most directly relevant study, asked samples of college students and members of the League of Women Voters to judge the frequency of thirty causes of death, having first given them an anchor (the annual death toll for motor vehicle accidents in the United States). While people's judgments were basically accurate, the study also showed systematic distortions: rare causes of death were overestimated and common causes underestimated; and accidents were judged to cause as many deaths as diseases, whereas diseases actually take about fifteen times as many lives. The earlier cited study by Combs and Slovic (1979) also reported a basic accuracy in perception: the correlation between public estimates of the annual mortality from 41 causes of death and the actual mortality associated with those causes was .94 (for ranked data) and .70 (for raw data). This was true despite the tendency of the two newspapers studied to overreport deaths from accidents and homicides and to underreport deaths caused by disease.

Similar findings have been reported by Warr (1980) about the relationship between official crime statistics and public perceptions of crime. Warr points out (p. 464) that there is a great deal of agreement between public perception and official information so far as ranking the frequency of crimes is concerned, but that respondents overestimated the official incidence of the least frequent offenses and underestimated the incidence of the most frequent offenses.

These findings do not imply that groups accurately perceive their own risk, however. Some surveys have found substantial discrepancies between the rate at which a group is victimized, and its fear of crime. Young black males, for example, report the largest number of victimizations and the smallest amount of fear, whereas older females (both black and white) report the highest level of fear and the lowest number of victimizations (Skogan, 1976; cited in Lewis and Salem, 1986:7). Although the reasons for these misperceptions are complex, the media are surmised to play a role by publicizing or failing to publicize the vulnerability of certain groups (cf. F. L. Cook, 1981; Kasperson et al., 1988; Slovic, 1987).

Two facts stand out from the findings of the studies above. First, public perceptions of risk are generally accurate, in the sense that conditions that cause a greater number of deaths tend to be perceived as doing so, and crimes occurring with greater frequency are also perceived as doing so. But, second, perceptions of risk are also inaccurate, in the sense that the risks of well-publicized hazards are always overestimated relative to those that are not well-publicized, and those that fail to receive attention are underestimated.

One theory of how the reporting of risk affects public opinion views these effects as occurring "at the margin," among those who have little knowledge about a hazard except for what comes to them by way of the mass media. This is also a plausible interpretation of media effects more generally (see Singer and Ludwig, 1987; Iyengar and Kinder, 1987). But, as the drop in European travel following some well-publicized terrorist attacks makes clear (see Chapter 1), such publicity can have dramatic behavioral consequences, at least in the short run. Thus, both overall public accuracy in risk perception, and the deviations related to media overcoverage of dramatic but relatively rare events, are important facts about the reporting and the perception of risk. Furthermore, we still know very little about how other media biases—for example, the emphasis on the new and the immediate—influence public perceptions.

CONCLUSION

One answer to the question posed in this chapter, Which hazards do the media feature and which do they ignore?, may be framed in terms of assumed audience interest. This explanation fits the pattern of results described, and it is the reason journalists give for why they cover some events and not others (see Nelkin, 1987; Schanberg, supra).[20]

In principle, various specialized media exist to satisfy the interests of diverse audiences. But when we looked at several such media in order to see whether their coverage of hazards reflected these interests, we found that with one exception they did not. In the first place, such magazines as *Ebony, Essence,* and *Ladies' Home Journal* carried virtually no stories about hazards during our sampling period, and none directed primarily at either women or blacks.[21] Nor did the *Amsterdam News* reflect the special interests of black readers, so far as hazard coverage was concerned, with one exception: coverage of the African famine, which was attended to more consistently and over a longer period of time by the *Amsterdam News* than by the other media in our sample.

In practice, then, the "assumed audience interest" principle may work more to limit coverage of the hazards of minority groups in the mass media than to amplify such coverage in the special press. Because of the small number of specialized media we looked at, and the short sampling period, our evidence for the assertion is limited, but we offer it as a hypothesis worth testing further.

A second possible answer to the question of which hazards the

---

[20]Note that much earlier, laboratory studies had demonstrated the influence of an anticipated audience on the kind and amount of material that is remembered (Zimmerman and Bauer, 1958).

[21]However, *Essence* has on occasion published award-winning reports on health and medical issues of special interest to African-Americans. This fact reveals the limitations of our research design, which sampled only four issues of each of the monthlies.

media feature and which they ignore may be stated in terms of the vested interests of specific powerful actors (e.g., the Union Carbide Company in Institute, West Virginia). Our study was not specifically designed to provide an answer to this question. However, our detailed analysis of the coverage of the MIC disaster in Bhopal, India, demonstrates the consequence of source-dependence on the part of reporters—a dependence which, in the area of risk-reporting, as in other areas, skews their perspective toward that of established institutions.[22]

Our analysis suggests that media coverage of hazards is similar to the coverage of other news. It focuses on individuals and events rather than on social and economic forces, on drama and conflict rather than on long-term conditions. Thus, in Weiss's words (1988), it presents "a superficial and fragmented view of reality." It is, in addition, a view biased by journalists' dependence on institutional sources, as well as by their assumptions about the media audience and its interests.

[22] Our study did not and could not (because of its design) provide evidence of conscious distortion or suppression of information by the media. However, the analysis of Weis and Burke (1987) suggests that the media, especially magazines, have ignored and even suppressed information about the harmful effects of smoking in deference to real or anticipated pressure from tobacco companies on whose advertising these media depend. See also Kessler (1989); Warner et al. (1992). Kessler notes, however, that the magazines did a reasonably good job of covering other kinds of cancer, including breast cancer. And some environmental groups may by now also have assumed the status of institutions.

4 / The Effect of Geographic Location on the Coverage of Hazards[1]

In this chapter we pursue the question of media bias, asking specifically whether the media devote too much or too little attention to hazards occurring in different parts of the world.

Two truisms pervade discussions of U.S. reporting of news from the Third World. The first contends that what gets reported is overwhelmingly bad news—nothing but "coups and earthquakes," in Rosenblum's phrase (1981). The second is captured by the adage which states, "One dead fireman in Brooklyn is worth five English bobbies, who are worth 50 Arabs, who are worth 500 Africans" (Boyer, 1985:18–21). The first implies that reports of natural and political disasters will outnumber reports of progress and stability in the news from Third World countries. The second implies that, all other things being equal, countries geographically or culturally close to us will get more play than countries far away in the reporting of disasters. Note that both of these truisms may actually be true: News about Country X (a

[1] An earlier version of this chapter, with Marc B. Glassman as a co-author, appeared as "Media Coverage of Disasters: The Effect of Geographic Location," *Journalism Quarterly* 68(1/2) (1991):48–58.

Third World country) may consist overwhelmingly of news about coups and earthquakes, but earthquakes in Country X may nevertheless get less play than earthquakes in the United States or a country close to the United States.

In 1986, two tests of the second hypothesis (that earthquakes or other natural disasters in Third World countries would get less play than those occurring elsewhere) were published in the *Journal of Communication*. One, by Gaddy and Tanjong (1986), concluded that region of the world contributed nothing to the prediction of the amount of time and space devoted to earthquake coverage in newspapers and television newscasts. The other, by Adams (1986), concluded that measures of a country's "closeness" to the U.S. did significantly improve prediction of the amount of time devoted to natural disasters on television. The present analysis involves yet another test of this hypothesis. We begin with a more detailed review of Adams and of Gaddy and Tanjong and then describe our test of the hypothesis that nearby disasters are treated as more newsworthy than those further away.

Gaddy and Tanjong (1986) examined 110 earthquakes occurring in 1982 and 1983 in countries all over the world. Sixty-six of these were covered by one or another of the three major television networks, the *New York Times,* or the London *Times*—many more by the print media than by the networks. Analyzing the effect of region (First World, Second World, and Third World), magnitude of earthquake, and numbers of dead and injured on the number of media reports, Gaddy and Tanjong found a statistically significant effect of numbers of dead and of physical damage, but no significant effect of region.[2] Thus, they rejected the hypothesis that the media attend disproportionately to earthquakes occurring in the Third World, once the risks associated with those events have been taken into account.

The second study, by Adams (1986), tested a somewhat different version of the same hypothesis—namely, that the media attend disproportionately to risks affecting groups perceived as culturally close. As we have already noted, the truth of this hypothesis is taken for granted by journalists.

---

[2] All the direct effects are small, ranging from 2–5 percent, but the total amount of variance explained by all the direct and indirect effects included in the model is about 25 percent.

Adams looked at how 30 major natural disasters of all types (earthquakes, floods, typhoons, etc.), each causing 300 deaths or more, were reported on television between 1972 and 1985. The estimated r^2 between disaster deaths and television coverage (measured in number of minutes) was .08. Substituting the logarithm of the number of deaths for the raw data increased Adams' estimate to .18, a figure which nevertheless explained less than one fifth of the variation in nightly network news attention. Seeking to account for the remainder, Adams tested a number of other explanatory variables, many of them suggested by previous theorists in this area (e.g., Epstein, 1973; Graber, 1980; Lichter, Rothman, and Lichter, 1986; and Roshco, 1975).

Adams found that three variables accounted for most of the variation in coverage (61 percent): the number of American tourists visiting the country, which he used as an indicator of social and cultural proximity; the logarithm of estimated disaster deaths; and geographical proximity. Thus, he concluded that instead of giving too much coverage to natural disaster stories from the Third World, as some researchers have charged, the press (more accurately, television) has actually given them proportionately too little attention, as measured by the number of deaths they cause.

In effect, both Adams and Gaddy and Tanjong ask whether country or region of the world contributes anything to explaining the variance in attention devoted to natural disasters, over and above the number of deaths and injuries they cause. Neither of them, however, tested the interaction between region and number of deaths, an interaction implied by the hypothesis. The present study provided another opportunity to put this hypothesis to the test.

Both Adams and Gaddy and Tanjong had access to an independent source of information about natural disasters (Gaddy and Tanjong, for all earthquakes occurring in 1982 and 1983; Adams, for all natural disasters responsible for 300 or more deaths occurring between 1972 and 1985), and their analyses involved a comparison of the press coverage received by each of these disasters. Lacking an independent source of information about our broad array of hazards, we substituted an analysis based on the media reports themselves, asking what determines the amount of coverage a hazard receives, once it has been selected for coverage at all. We examined three factors potentially influencing coverage: the number of fatalities associated with a specific instance of a hazard; whether or not the hazard is a new one; and in what region of the world the hazard occurred. We begin by looking at all six types of hazards, and then repeat the analysis for natural disasters only.

Because the news stories in our sample deal with a great variety of hazards that may themselves differ in news value, we control for the six types of hazard in all of the analyses that follow. This procedure of course does not control for specific hazards within any one type, and some of the variation we attribute to other variables may result from this imprecision. For example, stories about the 1984 Ethiopian famine dominated the natural hazards category, and stories about the methyl isocyanate leak in Bhopal dominated the category of materials hazards. Since these hazards also took place in specific countries, the findings about hazard type as well as geographic location are to some extent determined by the particular hazards occurring during this period of time. We attempt to deal with this problem by replicating the analyses for 1960, when no such extraordinary events occurred, and also by special weighting procedures described below.

THE EFFECT OF GEOGRAPHIC CLOSENESS

The news stories we monitored differed systematically in the likelihood with which they referred to the geographic location of the hazard. In both 1960 and 1984, stories about natural hazards were most likely to mention the place where the disaster had occurred (96.9 percent and 98.2 percent, respectively), followed by stories about energy hazards (96.3 percent and 94.3 percent). Stories about illness were least likely to do so, although the proportion of mentions was still high (74.2 percent and 69.7 percent). Stories about the other three hazards were intermediate between these points.

The location of those stories that mention place (as we have seen, the vast majority) is shown in Table 4.1 for 1960 and 1984, using broad categories comparable to those used by Adams (1986). Between 1960 and 1984, three noteworthy changes occurred. There was proportionately more news about hazards in the United

TABLE 4.1 / Geographic Location of Hazard Stories, by Year and Media[a]

Year and Media	N.Y.C. (%)	Other U.S. (%)	Europe (%)	South America (%)	Middle East (%)	Communist World (%)	Asia (%)	Africa, Third World (%)	(N)
1960:									
Daily	16.2	44.1	12.3	7.4	1.0	1.5	5.4	12.3	(204)
Weekly	11.6	52.2	15.9	0.0	4.3	0.0	4.3	11.6	(69)

$$\chi^2 = 11.67; \; df = 7; \; ns$$

Year and Media	N.Y.C. (%)	Other U.S. (%)	Europe (%)	South America (%)	Middle East (%)	Communist World (%)	Asia (%)	Africa, Third World (%)	(N)
1984:									
Daily	12.4	55.6	4.7	1.2	0.7	0.5	12.1	12.9	(428)
Weekly	—	69.5	1.7	1.7	0.8	0.0	11.9	14.4	(118)
TV	1.8	61.7	8.5	2.1	0.0	0.7	10.3	14.9	(282)

$$\chi^2 = 52.51; \; df = 14; \; p < .01.$$

[a]Based on stories that had a geographic focus. Differences between the 1960 and 1984 distributions are significant; $\chi^2 = 61.36; \; df = 7; \; p < .01.$

TABLE 4.2 / Prominence Given to Hazard Stories from Different Parts of the World, by Region and Year (Print Media Only)

Region	Percent Prominently Featured			
	1960		1984	
	(%)	(N)	(%)	(N)
New York City	9.8	(41)	11.3	(53)
Other United States	6.3	(126)	13.9	(320)
Europe	2.8	(36)	4.5	(22)
South America	6.7	(15)	0.0	(7)
Middle East	0.0	(5)	0.0	(4)
Communist World	33.3	(3)	0.0	(2)
Asia	0.0	(22)	21.5	(68)
Africa and Other Third World	4.2	(24)	19.4	(70)

States in 1984 than there had been in 1960. The sixties, it will be recalled, ushered in a period of increased awareness of vulnerability on the part of Americans: in the cities, where civil disorders flared; in relation to the environment; and, finally, in Vietnam. There was, on the other hand, less news about hazards in Europe in 1984 than there had been in 1960; and there were proportionately more stories about hazards in Asia in 1984 than there had been in 1960. Many of these stories dealt with the release of methyl isocyanate in Bhopal, India, in December 1984.

Table 4.1 also shows the location of 1984 hazard stories separately for print and television. As we would expect, television, a national medium, carried much less news about hazards in the New York metropolitan area. There was also somewhat more attention to Europe on TV than in print. Aside from these differences, the distributions are very similar.

In 1960, hazards in the U.S. were more likely to be featured prominently than those in other countries, with one apparent exception: one of the three stories about hazards in the Soviet Union was featured prominently (Table 4.2).[3] In 1984, hazards in Asia and Africa were most likely to be featured prominently, because

[3]The story was about Russian researchers' discovery of a new clue to the causes of cancer, which appeared on page 1 of the *Times*. It was, thus, not really a story about hazards *in* Russia.

TABLE 4.3 / Effect of Geographic Location, Hazard Type, and Number of Deaths on Space Devoted to Hazard Stories in Print Media, 1960

Independent Variable	Beta	Significance Level
Geographic location[a]	0.32	.000
Hazard type[b]	0.10	.406
Number of deaths	0.28	.000
Interaction cannot be computed		
	$R^2 = .154$	
	$N = 273$	
	$\overline{X} = 717$ (inches)	

[a]U.S. > Africa > Europe > Asia
[b]Natural = Materials > Complex > Energy > Benefit/Cost > Illness

stories about MIC (which has been described as the most serious industrial accident of all time) and about the Ethiopian famine dominated news from Asia and Africa during this period.

Besides looking at the prominence of hazard stories from different parts of the world, we also analyzed the amount of space or time devoted to them, again for both 1960 and 1984. In this analysis, we controlled simultaneously for type of hazard, associated number of deaths, and (for 1984 only) the newness of the hazard, using multiple classification analysis (MCA), a form of regression suitable for categorical independent variables.[4]

Table 4.3 summarizes the results of an MCA analysis for 1960. The table displays the significance of the F-values associated with hazard type, geographic location,[5] and number of deaths[6] associated with each hazardous event, as well as the betas associated with the main effects, and the overall explained variance. Both geographic location and number of deaths had a significant effect

[4]Analyses reported in the preceding chapter indicate that both numbers of deaths and injuries and the newness of the hazard were correlated with story length.

[5]For these analyses, we combined stories about South America with those about Europe, and stories about the Middle East and the Communist world with those about Asia. As can be seen from Table 4.1, there were very few stories about the two former regions in the sample, but the findings for "Asia" may be somewhat ambiguous because of this strategy.

[6]To preserve non-zero cells, we collapsed this variable into three categories: 0 = no mention, 1 = less than 10, 2 = more than 10.

on the space devoted to hazard stories in the print media in 1960; hazard type did not. Because of the small number of cases, it was not possible to test for the presence of an interaction effect. The total variance explained by these two variables is 15.4 percent.[7]

Though no highly dramatic event, such as Bhopal or the African famine, dominated the news in 1960, stories about hazards in Africa and other Third World countries were longer, on average, than stories about hazards in any other part of the world except the United States, even controlling (roughly) for the number of associated deaths. Stories about Asia, however, were shorter than other stories.[8]

The same analysis was performed for hazard stories in 1984, but here the results are more complicated. They are shown in Table 4.4 for print, with column inches as the dependent variable, and in Table 4.5 for television, with number of lines in the television news script as the dependent variable.

Panel A of Tables 4.4 and 4.5 shows the results of an equation including only two independent variables (hazard type and geographic location) and their interaction; and Panel B adds the number of deaths and a variable indicating whether or not the hazard, in our judgment, was a new one. But if we look at Column 1, three differences from the 1960 results immediately become apparent. First, in 1984, hazard type had a significant effect on space in the print media, whereas geographic location did not. Second, the interaction between geographic location and hazard type is significant for both print and television. And third, the amount of variance explained, even by all four independent variables, is less than the amount explained for 1960. It is also less for print than for television.

As we have already indicated, the significant interactions in 1984 reflect the disproportionate attention given to materials hazards in Asia and to natural hazards in Africa, and these, in turn,

---

[7] The total variance explained by a model containing only geographic location and hazard type explained a modest 8 percent of the variance.

[8] As already noted, "Asia" is a heterogeneous category. Some of its countries are culturally and geographically distant but economically advanced—for example, Japan and Taiwan—and others are not only culturally distant but economically disadvantaged—for example, Vietnam and Cambodia. Furthermore, China and the Soviet Union are also included among "Asian" countries. Thus, it is particularly difficult to interpret the meaning of length of stories about hazards in Asia.

TABLE 4.4 / Effect of Geographic Location, Hazard Type, Number of Deaths, and Newness of Hazard on Space Devoted to Hazard Stories in Print Media, 1984

	Column 1		Column 2		Column 3	
	Beta	Sig.	Beta	Sig.	Beta	Sig.
A.						
Hazard type	0.27	.000	Hazard type[c] 0.17	.005	Hazard type[d] 0.18	.002
Geographic location	0.13	ns[a]	Geographic location 0.17	.007	Geographic location 0.18	.003
Interaction		.052	Interaction	ns	Interaction	ns
	$R^{2b} = .065$		$R^2 = .064$		$R^2 = .064$	
	$N = 546$		$N = 432$		$N = 441$	
	$\bar{x} = 11.92$		$\bar{x} = 11.14$		$\bar{x} = 11.30$	
	$R^2 = 0.096$		$R^2 = .078$		$R^2 = .081$	
B.						
Hazard type	0.28	.000	Hazard type[c] 0.19	.009	Hazard type[d] 0.20	.004
Geographic location	0.14	.078	Geographic location 0.19	.002	Geographic location 0.21	.001
Number of deaths	0.20	.000	Number of deaths 0.12	.056	Number of deaths 0.14	.023
Newness of hazard	0.00	ns	Newness of hazard 0.03	ns	Newness of hazard 0.03	ns
Interactions cannot be computed			Interactions cannot be computed		Interactions cannot be computed	
	$R^2 = 0.096$		$R^2 = .078$		$R^2 = .081$	

[a] "ns" means $p > .10$, usually substantially greater.
[b] Exclusive of interactions. Where applicable, R^2 and betas are based on three-category Deaths variable, although two-category variable was used to test interactions.
[c] Stories about MIC explosion in Bhopal and famine in Ethiopia eliminated.
[d] Stories about MIC explosion and Ethiopia famine reweighted. See text.

TABLE 4.5 / Effect of Geographic Location, Hazard Type, Number of Deaths, and Newness of Hazard on Time Devoted to Hazard Stories on Television, 1984

	Column 1		Column 2		Column 3	
	Beta	Sig.	Beta	Sig.	Beta	Sig.
A. Hazard type	0.15	ns[a]	Hazard type[b] 0.10	ns	Hazard type[c] 0.11	ns
Geographic location	0.41	.000	0.09	ns	0.24	.013
Interaction		.048	Interaction	ns	Interaction	ns
	$R^2 = .131$		$R^2 = .023$		$R^2 = .056$	
	$N = 282$		$N = 216$		$N = 222$	
	$\bar{x} = 25.24$		$\bar{x} = 22.36$		$\bar{x} = 22.92$	
B. Hazard type	0.10	ns	Hazard type[b] 0.08	ns	Hazard type[c] 0.07	ns
Geographic location	0.35	.000	0.08	ns	0.20	.055
Number of deaths	0.15	.053	0.17	.073	0.15	.110
Newness of hazard	0.10	ns	0.14	.074	0.13	.087
Interactions cannot be computed			Interactions cannot be computed		Interactions cannot be computed	
	$R^2 = .138$		$R^2 = .057$		$R^2 = .088$	

[a] "ns" means $p > .10$, usually substantially greater.
[b] Stories about MIC explosion in Bhopal and famine in Ethiopia eliminated.
[c] Stories about MIC explosion in Bhopal and Ethiopian famine reweighted. See text.

largely reflect two specific hazardous events, in two specific places: MIC in Bhopal and famine in Ethiopia. In order to eliminate the effect of these specific hazards, we show, in Tables 4.4 and 4.5, the results of two alternative sets of equations. The first, in Column 2, eliminates all stories dealing with either of these two specific hazards altogether. The second, in Column 3, includes randomly selected stories dealing with both hazards, but includes only as many stories about each one as the average number of stories about a particular hazard in each of the two hazard categories.[9]

For stories in newspapers and magazines (see Table 4.4), correcting for the overrepresentation of MIC and Ethiopian famine stories eliminates the significance of the two-way interaction and restores the significance of geographic location. All main effects except newness are now significant in all equations.

Despite the elimination or sharp reduction of MIC and famine stories in Columns 2 and 3, the ordering of categories remains largely unchanged (MCA output, not shown). For example, stories about materials hazards get more space than those devoted to illness, which in turn get more than natural hazards, which get more than energy hazards. Stories which mentioned more than ten deaths get more space than stories with one to ten deaths, which get more than those with no mention of death. And hazard stories about Africa get more space than stories about the U.S., which in turn get more than stories about Europe, which get more than stories about Asia.[10] Except for the reversal of attention to the United States and Africa, all this is very similar to the results for 1960.

Thus, for print media, the effect of reducing or eliminating the importance of specific highly dramatic events is to reduce the total variance explained, but influences on the ordering of categories are small or nonexistent. The effect of geographic location is simi-

---

[9]Even this strategy includes too many stories about these two specific hazardous events, because the different hazards within a category ordinarily represent more than one event. Thus, there may be five stories about tornadoes, but they are not necessarily all about the same tornado. With respect to MIC and the famine, however, most (though not all) stories deal with the same event.
[10]In the equations with the original version of the hazard variable, however (Column 1 in Table 4.4), stories about hazards in Asia get more space than those about hazards in Europe.

lar for print media in 1960 and 1984, though the attention devoted
to different hazard types has changed in the interim. The effect,
furthermore, is different from that predicted on the basis of Adams's work: Africa gets much more attention, in our analysis,
than we would expect on the basis of his study.

Like the print media, television coverage shows certain changes
depending on whether the specific, highly dramatic hazards of
MIC and famine are allowed to carry their natural weight or
whether this weight is reduced or eliminated in an attempt to
render the findings more generalizable (see Table 4.5).

When stories about MIC and the Ethiopian famine carry their
natural weight (Column 1 of Table 4.5), we note that in the sim-
plest form of the equation, hazard type has no significant effect,
but both geographic location and the interaction between hazard
and location do. As additional variables are added, we lose the
ability to test for an interaction effect; however, hazard type and
newness remain insignificant while geographic location and number of deaths retain their significance. As in the print media, the
longest stories are those about Africa, but stories about Asia are
now next to those on Africa in length. The overall variance explained increases slightly, from 13.1 percent to 13.8 percent, once
all the variables are in the equation.

However, when, in Columns 2 and 3, we attempt to reduce the
impact of two idiosyncratic, visually dramatic hazardous events,
the total amount of variance explained becomes trivial and very
few of the individual variables remain statistically significant. We
interpret this result as indicating that television news is news
about specific dramatic events, and that it is more difficult to predict average television coverage on the basis of hazard type or
geographic location than it is to predict print coverage.

Even for print media, however, the total amount of variance
explained by all the variables we are able to measure is very small;
most of the variance appears to be accounted for by variables
we did not conceptualize or measure. Gaddy and Tanjong, and
Adams, on the other hand, were able, on the basis of a small
number of variables, to predict a relatively large share of the variance in news coverage received by a series of natural disasters.

We next attempted to approximate these analyses more closely
by restricting our own to the category of natural disasters. When

TABLE 4.6 / Effect of Geographic Location and Number of Deaths on Space and Time Devoted to Hazard Stories, 1960 and 1984 (Natural Hazards Only)

| | | Column 1 | | Column 2[a] | |
		Beta	Significance	Beta	Significance
A.	1960 Print				
	Geographic location	0.44	.004	Does not apply	
	Number of deaths	0.32	.037		
	Interaction		ns		
		$R^2 = .275$			
		$N = 61$			
		$\bar{x} = 7.34$			
B.	1984 Print				
	Geographic location	0.33	.018	0.44	.045
	Number of deaths	0.23	ns	0.26	ns
	Interaction		ns		ns
		$R^2 = .124$		$R^2 = .237$	
		$N = 102$		$N = 50$	
		$\bar{x} = 10.73$		$\bar{x} = 10.38$	
C.	1984 Television				
	Geographic location	0.46	.003	0.68	.022
	Number of deaths	0.26	.068	0.46	.048
	Interaction		ns		ns
		$R^2 = .326$		$R^2 = .351$	
		$N = 65$		$N = 34$	
		$\bar{x} = 29.86$		$\bar{x} = 23.74$	

[a]Stories about Ethiopian famine reweighted. See text.

this is done, the results confirm our expectation that it is easier to predict coverage within a hazard category than across categories (Table 4.6). For print coverage of natural disasters in 1960, number of deaths and geographic location together explain 27.5 percent of the variance in the space 61 stories give to 10 different kinds of natural disasters. Natural disasters occurring in the United States get more space, on average, than those occurring in Africa, which get more than those in Europe, which get more than those in Asia. And natural disaster stories that mention more deaths get more space than those that mention fewer or none at all.

For natural disasters in 1984, the explained variance also increases: to 35.1 percent for television and 23.7 percent for the print media, when the data are weighted to reduce the effect of the

Ethiopian famine (Table 4.6). None of the interactions between number of deaths and geographic location is significant. However, the effect of number of deaths is curvilinear for both print and television.

The variance explained in our analysis of natural disasters coverage, though less than Adams's, is comparable to that explained by Gaddy and Tanjong. However, our findings concerning the role of geographic location differ from those of the other two studies. Unlike Gaddy and Tanjong, we found the effect of geographic location to be significant. But unlike Adams, we found that hazards in Africa get much more coverage than would be predicted on the basis of closeness. Both in the reweighted 1984 print sample and in the unweighted and reweighted television samples, stories about natural disasters in Africa were longer than those about other countries. And even in the unweighted print sample, stories about natural disasters in Africa were second only to those about such disasters in the U.S. in length. As we have seen, the same was true of natural disaster stories in 1960.

We are tempted to conclude from this that Adams and conventional journalistic wisdom are wrong—that deaths in Africa are as newsworthy as deaths in the United States. But because our control for number of deaths was very crude, we decided to examine the mean number of deaths associated with natural disasters in each of the four regions we distinguished. Means were calculated from a nine-category scale running from 0 (no mention of deaths) to 8 (1 billion deaths). By far the largest number of stories made no mention of deaths at all, but the results do not change in any significant way when we calculate the average number of deaths for only those stories in which there is any mention of deaths.

Mean number of deaths by region is shown in Table 4.7. When we rank the four regions with respect to the number of deaths and the length of natural disaster stories, our conclusions remain largely intact. In 1960, the average number of deaths, as measured by our nine-point scale, increased from 1.22 for print stories about natural disasters in the U.S. to 1.48 for stories about such disasters in Europe to 1.75 for stories about natural disasters in Asia, but then dropped to 0.36 for stories about natural disasters in Africa, which nevertheless were second only to stories about the U.S. in length. The same ordering is maintained if we look at stories about

TABLE 4.7 / **Mean Number of Deaths in Hazard Stories from Different Parts of the World, by Media, Year, and Ranked Story Length (R) (Natural Hazards Only)**

Region									

Region	R	Print	(N)	R	Print	(N)	R	TV	(N)
		Mean Number of Deaths[a] and Ranked Length (R)							
		1960			1984			1984	
U.S.	1	1.22	(18)	2	0.50	(26)	3	0.21	(24)
Europe	3	1.48	(21)	4	0.67	(3)	0	0.00	(0)
Asia	4	1.75	(8)	3	2.33	(6)	2	0.40	(5)
Africa	2	0.36	(14)	1	1.85	(67)	1	1.81	(36)

[a]Computed from a nine-point scale running from 0 (no mention of deaths) to 8 (1 billion deaths). The number of deaths was coded from the news stories themselves.

all hazards, not just natural disasters, and if we look only at stories which include *any* mention of deaths.

In 1984, both in print and on television, the mean number of deaths in stories about natural disasters in Africa far exceeded the mean number of deaths in stories about such disasters in Europe or the United States (Table 4.7). Stories about Africa were also longer than stories about natural hazards in those countries. Television stories about natural hazards in Asia were second only to those on Africa in length, and the number of deaths in those stories was also second to those in Africa. But print stories about natural disasters in Asia, which involved a larger average number of deaths than stories about such disasters in any other part of the world, were shorter than other stories except those about Europe.[11]

What conclusions do we draw from these analyses?

First, unlike Gaddy and Tanjong, we find that geographic location, along with number of deaths and (marginally) newness of the hazard, does influence the space and time devoted to natural disasters in the press.

Second, unlike Adams, we do not find a neat relationship between length, geographic location, and number of deaths. In 1960,

[11]If we consider only those stories in which any mention of death occurred (i.e., when stories with zero deaths are excluded), deaths in Africa exceed those in Asia for stories about natural hazards and all hazards combined, and stories about Africa exceed those about all other places in length.

stories about natural disasters in the United States and Africa were longer than warranted by their number of deaths, but stories about Europe and, especially, Asia were shorter. In 1984, the length of stories about natural disasters in Africa was appropriate to the number of deaths they contained, but stories about Asia were too short and those about the United States were too long. Thus, we would modify Adams's conclusion to say that news about hazards in the United States is given disproportionately too much attention in the U.S. press; but there are no consistent biases in favor of other parts of the world.[12]

This conclusion is buttressed, at least in the case of natural hazards, by the absence of a statistically significant interaction in any of our analyses between the effects of geographic location and number of deaths on story length.

Third, neither our study nor the two earlier ones shed any light on whether news from the Third World is predominantly bad news. A test of this hypothesis would require comparing the proportion of "good news" and "bad news" stories about African and other Third World countries with those about other parts of the world. None of the three studies cited carried out such a comparison, and of course it would be virtually impossible to assess the actual, real-world proportion of "good events" versus "bad events" occurring in each of those parts of the world.

Is it possible to reconcile the differences among these three studies?

It is important to note that the three differ in the methods they use. Adams's study is limited to television coverage and to natural disasters causing at least 300 deaths. There is a fairly small number of these, 30, and they occurred over a period of fourteen years. Gaddy and Tanjong used a larger number of more restricted events (110 earthquakes) occurring in a shorter period of time (1982 and 1983), and with no lower limit on the number of deaths. Furthermore, they used number of stories, rather than story length, as their dependent variable. Our study had no independent source of information about disasters, but instead analyzed the press coverage of all types of hazards appearing over a period

---

[12]See also a study by Bridges (1989), which concludes that proximity is much more important in the hypothetical situation than in the actual case.

of several months in 1960 and 1984. And, like Adams, we used story length as the dependent variable. We have, of course, no way of knowing whether the effect of many short stories on public awareness is equivalent to that of a few long ones, nor do we know the correlation between story frequency and story length.

Given these differences in methods, the differences in findings are perhaps not surprising. And none of these methods is ideal for testing the hypothesis.

In concluding this chapter, we would like to make explicit what has remained largely implicit so far. "Bias" in the media is often the unintended consequence of attention to news values. And news values, in turn, have to do with audience interest—either as measured through reader/viewer surveys or else as assumed. When news values are assumed rather than measured, they may reflect the bias of journalists. But even careful measurement is no guarantee against the "biased" interests of the media audience. The analyses in Chapters 3 and 4 have shown the existence of three such "biases": in favor of hazards associated with a large number of deaths; in favor of new hazards; and in favor of hazards occurring in the United States.

5 / Information About Hazards: Their Benefits and Costs[1]

In the preceding chapters we tried to answer questions of selection and emphasis—what sorts of hazards the media feature, which they ignore, and what determines the amount of coverage hazards get once a decision has been made to cover them at all. In this chapter, we turn to a different set of questions, asking what kind of information the mass media include in news stories about hazards.

The media, we found, select for emphasis hazards that are relatively serious and relatively rare. It is the combination that gives them their punch. But by singling them out for attention, the media make them more "available" for recall by the public, thus leading, by psychological laws spelled out by Tversky and Khaneman (1973), to overestimation of the frequency of their occurrence.

One of the most dramatic instances of the operation of these media and perceptual laws is the case of toxic shock syndrome (TSS).[2] In four months, according to Weiner (1986), TSS, until

[1] An edited version of this chapter appeared as "Reporting Hazards: Their Benefits and Costs," *Journal of Communication* 37(3) (1987):10–26.

[2] Here, we treat the disease as the hazard. But note that one could also regard tampons as the hazard, with an associated probability of causing toxic shock.

then a virtually unknown disease, brought about a multimillion dollar recall of Rely tampons. In 1985 the *New York Times* reported that, in the four-and-a-half years since TSS had burst into public awareness, reaction to the disease had caused significant changes in women's tampon-buying habits.[3]

Yet the statistics of the disease alone hardly warranted such a reaction. Weiner notes that about 5,000 cases, or about 9 for every 100,000 menstruating women, are estimated to occur annually: "a notable public health threat, but a very rare one," about equal in frequency to tuberculosis at that time. But, as he points out, "Conveying to the public that a new disease is very serious but very infrequent is a difficult task" (p. 158).

The reason for the lack of congruence between the risk and the amount of media attention it receives lies in the man-bites-dog nature of news. A rare hazard is more newsworthy than a common one, other things being equal. A new hazard is more newsworthy than an old one. And a dramatic hazard—one that kills many people at once, suddenly or mysteriously—is more newsworthy than a long-familiar illness.

As we have seen, the amount of media attention to a hazard (as measured by the number of news stories) appears to be unrelated to the number of deaths it causes per year. That fact alone, we argue, poses a serious obstacle to the accurate perception of risk. Still, in the body of the story journalists may provide the information needed to form accurate estimates: the likelihood that a hazard will occur, and the likelihood that it will cause harm.[4]

In the remainder of this chapter, therefore, we first examine the quality and quantity of the information the media in our sample provided—or failed to provide—about risks associated with hazards in the news. But, since no behavior is risk-free, framing discussions of hazards without attention either to their benefits or to the costs of alternative actions is potentially misleading, especially

---

[3] Weiner reports that subsequent epidemiological studies did not bear out the initial linkage of TSS with Rely tampons but instead implicated all superabsorbent tampons. According to Weiner, a 1985 Harvard study strongly suggested that magnesium absorption by superabsorbent fibers encouraged toxin production by staph bacteria, and the remaining super tampons on the market were redesigned to take this into account.

[4] For example, news stories may provide information about the likelihood that a person will develop cancer in a given year, and the probability of dying from the disease; the number of fires a year, and the proportion resulting in fatalities.

when benefits or alternatives are not widely known. No one, presumably, needs to be reminded about the virtues of the automobile. But the benefits of ethylene dibromide (EDB) are perhaps less familiar.[5] Accordingly, in addition to inquiring about risks, we also asked what kind of information was provided about related benefits, and, in particular, how much information there was about the ratio of benefits to costs. Finally, we consider whether or not any discussion was included about alternatives to the hazard in question, and about the benefits and costs associated with these alternatives. We also ask whether this information varies according to the type of media—newspapers, newsmagazines, and television—involved.

INFORMATION ABOUT RISK

To anticipate the conclusion that emerges from our detailed analysis: The media do not report on risks; they report on *harms*. To be more precise, as Herbert Gans has pointed out to us, they report on tornadoes, floods, politics, gas explosions, and midair collisions, from which we have abstracted concepts such as risk and harm. Ordinarily, journalists do not intend to report on such abstract concepts at all. But this does not prevent us from looking at what is reported from a different perspective, in search of potentially unanticipated consequences.

Most news stories about hazards do include some information about associated harms (by which we mean property damage, illness, injury, and death). Some information about deaths, for example, was given in 49.1 percent of news stories in our 1960 sample, and 50.4 percent of stories in 1984; and some information about injuries appeared in 25.4 percent of 1960 stories in which injury was a possible outcome, and in 39.0 percent of those in

---

[5]Fischhoff (1985), among others, has noted that the public was ill-informed about the likely consequences of banning EDB, both in terms of possible alternative chemicals and in terms of higher food prices. More recently, discussions of the risk of silicone breast implants have referred to saline implants as an alternative, with no consideration of the possible risks these pose. (See, e.g., Philip J. Hilts, "FDA Restricts Use of Implants Pending Studies," *New York Times*, April 17, 1992, p. 1.)

1984.[6] Almost 90 percent and 75 percent, respectively, of the stories that mentioned deaths or injuries in 1960 actually gave the number of people who had died or been injured *in that incident*, and the same was true of 77.7 percent and 62.3 percent of stories in 1984.[7]

But while inclusion of these numbers conveys some sense of the seriousness of the hazard (i.e., of the likelihood of its causing harm, given its occurrence), they do not give readers or viewers any inkling of how likely the hazard is to occur. For that, baseline information is needed: How many fires occur each year, and what percentage of these involve fatalities? How many people are killed in automobile accidents each year? How many cases of toxic shock syndrome are reported each year, and how many result in death? How often has a transplant operation succeeded?

It might be argued that the annual mortality associated with a hazard is the *minimum* information needed in order to form some conception of the size of the risk it poses.[8] Yet for many hazards, this requirement is not easily met.

In the first place, the information may simply not be known. While it is possible to count the number of cancer deaths per year, it is not possible, in any straightforward fashion, to say how many of them are attributable to the use of saccharin, for example. Estimating the number of deaths attributable to most materials hazards requires making assumptions about the effects of estimated exposures on humans—assumptions and estimates that may not

[6]The total number of stories for which mention of deaths was coded was 842 in 1984 and 284 in 1960. For injuries, the number was 808 in 1984 and 269 in 1960. Mention of deaths or injuries was not coded for the category of chronic and acute illness, though we did code prevalence, incidence, the probability of death given the occurrence of illness, and the annual mortality associated with the disease.

[7]We did not attempt to verify the accuracy of these figures. A study by Scanlon, Luukko, and Morton (1978) found that press coverage of six Canadian crises left a generally accurate impression of the events but erred on some of the details. They fault the newspapers for including unattributed information in their accounts (all the errors were unattributed), and for not informing readers of the uncertainty surrounding some of the figures in the stories.

[8]For some hazards, such as nuclear power, Slovic, Fischhoff, and Lichtenstein (1979) argue that risk perceptions are based on conceptions of the maximum potential mortality associated with a single disaster, rather than annual mortality. And measures of potential, rather than actual, deaths might well be needed in order to give some idea of the riskiness of newly introduced materials hazards, such as aspartame.

be correct, and for which there may be no good way to model the size of the error.[9] Writing about risk assessment in the *New York Times* of January 2, 1983, David Schribman notes that although scientists have made great strides, "they recognize that the technique is still more of an art than a science and that many uncertainties remain," a position echoed by Freudenberg in an article in *Science* in 1988. And Schribman quotes Beverly R. Paigen, a former consultant for the carcinogen risk assessment group at the Environmental Protection Agency (EPA) and an adviser to the residents of the Love Canal neighborhood in upper New York state: "Risk assessment only deals with what we know," she said. "At Love Canal we had knowledge of what those chemicals do to workers on the job. We had no knowledge of what they do to pregnant women in the home. There are still very few chemicals for which we know enough to come out with a risk assessment . . . (for) the general population."

Second, even when the information is available—as it is for many natural hazards, energy hazards, and illnesses—it may not be easily available in the most meaningful form. For example, in order to appraise the risks associated with skiing, one would want to know not how many deaths are caused by skiing each year but how many of them occur among skiers—undoubtedly a much larger fraction. Attempting to provide such information, Michael de Courcy Hinds, writing in the January 14, 1989, *New York Times*, notes, "Ski industry statistics are sketchy, but the resort industry said that about 100 injuries occur for every 10,000 skier visits, including about 6 head injuries."[10]

Sometimes, indeed, risk information is presented superbly in the press, for example, as in a *New York Times* report of December

[9]Hohenemser et al. (1983) argue that their hazard descriptors may be useful in estimating the risk of newly discovered hazards by disclosing the similarity in their structure to those which are better known. But their descriptors themselves involved many estimates and assumptions.

[10]Even when good information is presented appropriately, research has shown that perception will vary depending on how the information is presented—on the words used, and on their context (Sirken, 1986). Fischhoff (1979) notes that many of these biasing effects have been known since the beginnings of experimental psychology in the mid-1800s. And Tversky and Khaneman (1981) have shown that for many different kinds of choices the way a problem is "framed" can affect the outcome.

18, 1987, on a U.S. Department of Transportation study of the effect on traffic fatalities of raising the speed limit on rural interstate roads. But even this Associated Press story neglects to provide any information about the benefits of increased speed (or, conversely, the costs of reducing the speed limit). Another example of good reporting on risk is a story by Philip M. Boffey on page 1 of the *Times* of April 22, 1988, on the risks of contracting AIDS under various conditions. While Boffey presents the risk estimates calculated by the authors of the study, he also interviews a number of other scientists about the accuracy of their assumptions, calculations, and conclusions.[11]

In order to quantify the inclusion of risk information in our sample of hazard stories, we asked, for each story analyzed in detail, whether or not information was given about the annual mortality associated with the hazard. For natural, energy, and materials hazards and for illness we also asked whether or not information was given about the size of the population at risk. And for natural, energy, and materials hazards we asked, as well, about the spatial extent of the hazard, whether or not there was any delay in the onset of consequences, how long the risk associated with the hazard persisted, and whether or not the hazard affected more than one generation.[12]

As can be seen from Table 5.1, only 7 percent of the stories in 1960—11 out of 156—carried any information about the annual mortality associated with the hazard. The number was even lower (5 percent, or 31 stories out of 624) in 1984. There was little variation by type of hazard, except that stories about natural hazards were especially unlikely to include this kind of information, and stories about activities involving benefits and costs were especially likely to do so.

---

[11] Another excellent example of risk reporting, this time in a scholarly journal, is Gale (1987).

[12] These six were selected from the twelve descriptors employed by Hohenemser et al. (1983) to characterize technological hazards in general. The other six are: intentionality, concentration, recurrence, maximum human mortality, and nonhuman mortality (experienced and potential). In our pilot work, these dimensions were never referred to in news stories about hazards, and we therefore did not systematically monitor references to them. Most of the others have been found, in experimental work, to affect subjective ratings of risk (see Slovic, 1987).

TABLE 5.1 / **Percentage of Issues[a] Stories Giving Information about Dimensions of Hazardousness, by Year**

Dimension of Hazardousness	1960		1984	
	% Making Reference[b] (%) (N)	% Giving Quantitative Information (%) (N)	% Making Reference (%) (N)	% Giving Quantitative Information (%) (N)
Annual mortality[c]	7.1 (156)	72.7 (11)	5.0 (624)	90.3 (31)
Population at risk[d]	7.1 (140)	80.0 (10)	24.2 (483)	89.7 (117)
Spatial extent	17.8 (101)	100.0 (18)	19.8 (373)	100.0 (74)
Delay	3.0 (100)	66.7 (3)	2.7 (373)	50.0 (10)
Persistence	8.9 (101)	88.9 (9)	8.4 (371)	68.8 (32)
Transgenerational effects	2.0 (100)	DNA	4.3 (373)	DNA

[a]Dimensions of hazardousness were coded only for stories dealing with some risk issues (i.e., not for event-only stories or for those making no mention of risk). There were 157 issue stories in 1960 and 624 in 1984.
[b]Differences between 1960 and 1984 are significant only for the number of stories making reference to the population at risk ($\chi^2 = 19.51$; $df = 1$; $p < .01$).
[c]Coded only for natural disasters, energy hazards, materials hazards, and illness.
[d]Coded only for natural, energy, and materials hazards.

With some exceptions, information about the other dimensions of hazardousness was given even less frequently (see Table 5.1).[13] Information about the size of the population at risk appeared in 7 percent of relevant stories in 1960 but in a much larger fraction—24.2 percent—of 1984 stories, mainly because this information was given in 52 percent of stories about natural hazards, up from 25 percent in 1960. And information about the spatial extent of the hazard appeared in almost one fifth of the stories in both

[13]As indicated earlier, for chronic and acute illnesses we coded information about incidence, prevalence, and the probability of death, given the occurrence of illness. The proportions of news stories giving such items of information ranged from 7.5 percent to 16 percent. With one exception, there was no difference between 1984 and 1960. The single exception was prevalence, mentioned in 40 percent of illness stories in 1984, an increase largely accounted for by the tendency to give the prevalence of AIDS cases.

1960 and 1984, again largely because of the inclusion of this kind of information in stories about natural hazards.[14]

The information discussed so far simply involves a reference to a particular hazard dimension. The number of stories containing quantitative estimates of the annual mortality, the size of the population at risk, and so on, was of course even smaller. In 1960, for example, 3 of the 11 stories with a reference to annual mortality contained a qualitative reference only, as did 3 of 31 such stories in 1984.[15] The percentage of hazard stories containing quantitative references to the various hazard dimensions is shown in columns 2 and 4 of Table 5.1. Thus, while almost all news stories mentioned some harms associated with a particular hazard, virtually none of them gave readers or viewers a way of assessing the likelihood that that harm would occur. Virtually none, that is, gave readers or viewers a way of assessing risk. Friedman (1991:80) writes about press performance after Three Mile Island: "To a reader or viewer trying to decide whether to pack his bags and run, radiation reports in the media were often as useless as a baseball score of 6–4 that neglected to mention which teams had played. The Task Force [charged with evaluating media performance] found that the reporters covering TMI had made improper comparisons and factually impossible statements, as well as providing insufficient background information." And then, commenting on her own study of media coverage of the risk of radon, she notes: "A public opinion poll we did showed that, although people had been alerted to radon's dangers by the local newspapers' coverage, they could not evaluate clearly whether they were at risk because they did not understand the terms or concepts involved" (p. 81).

Because risk information is given so rarely, we do not analyze

---

[14]Concepts such as the size of the population at risk and the spatial extent of the hazard are obviously incorporated much more easily into certain kinds of news stories than others (e.g., stories about natural disasters and certain kinds of materials hazards).

[15]For example, "Doctors have found a way to repair the hearts of children born without a left ventricle, the main pumping chamber, and save them from a common birth defect that until now has always been fatal" (*New York Times*, Jan. 6, 1983). There is no indication of what "common" means. For an ingenious attempt to quantify such words as "large," "often," "seldom," and the like, see Bradburn and Miles (1979).

the form it takes when it is provided. But that form is likely to have important consequences. For example, Fischhoff (1985) notes that the risks of a drug seemed much worse when described in relative terms ("a doubling of your chances of a stroke") than in absolute terms ("an increase of 1 in 80,000 per year in your chance of dying from a stroke"). He and his colleagues recommended that both formulations be included in drug inserts. Or, to take another example, the lifetime risk of being in an automobile accident can act as a potent incentive for the use of seatbelts, since it is appreciably higher than the risk associated with any single trip (McKean, 1985:30).

INFORMATION ABOUT BENEFITS AND COSTS

Proportion of Story Devoted to Benefits and Costs[16]

Although actual or potential harms were almost always mentioned in a news story, information about benefits was included much less often. We coded the following as benefits: reduce property damage; reduce illness; reduce injury; reduce deaths; enhance quality of life; other. The first four correspond to the risks coded for each hazard; the next-to-last includes economic benefits. We did not code the mention of benefits for illnesses and natural disasters.

Especially in 1960, we found that relatively few stories in our study mentioned any benefits at all. By contrast, all but a tiny fraction of hazard stories—3.2 percent in 1984 and 6.5 percent in 1960—made some mention of associated harms. Benefits were mentioned in 18.2 percent of all stories in 1960, but in proportionately twice as many—38.8 percent—in 1984. In both years, news stories about materials hazards and complex technologies were much more likely to discuss benefits than those about energy hazards or activities involving benefits and costs (Table 5.2). In fact, by 1984 almost half (44.9 percent) of such stories made some mention of associated benefits. This fact, plus the increase in such stories between 1960 and 1984, largely accounts for the more frequent mention of benefits in 1984.

---

[16]We have used the terms "cost" and "harm" synonymously, even though the costs of a hazard include more than its potential harm to life and property.

TABLE 5.2 / Proportion of Story Devoted to Benefits,[a] by Year

Proportion	1960[b] Energy[c] (%)	1960[b] Materials[d] (%)	1984 Energy (%)	1984 Materials (%)
No mention	84.6	77.8	73.8	55.1
Less than ¼	13.5	13.9	18.7	27.5
¼–½	2.0	8.3	6.7	11.6
½–¾	0.0	0.0	0.7	5.0
More than ¾	0.0	0.0	0.0	0.7
(N)	(52)	(36)	(134)	(276)

$$X^2 = 2.12, df = 2, ns \qquad X^2 = 15.98, df = 4, \\ p < .01$$

[a] Information about benefits was coded for issue stories only (see fn. a, Table 5.1). Such information was not coded for natural disasters or illnesses.
[b] Differences between 1960 and 1984 are significant for materials hazards but not for energy hazards.
[c] Includes activities involving benefits and costs.
[d] Includes complex technologies.

However, when benefits were mentioned, they generally (75 percent of the time in 1960 and 64 percent in 1984) made up less than a quarter of the story. By contrast, both in 1960 and in 1984, only about one third of hazard stories devoted less than a quarter of their space to a discussion of harm, and 21 percent devoted more than three quarters of their space to such a discussion. This is true even though benefits were defined somewhat more inclusively than harms. In part, of course, this is because we were looking for hazard stories; in part, however, it may reflect the nature of what is defined as news.

What is true at an aggregate level is true, as well, for individual stories. In 1960 there was no single story, among those dealing with energy hazards or benefit-cost activities, in which the proportion of space given to the benefits of a hazard was equal to the proportion of space given to its harms. And even among materials hazards, this was true of only 8.3 percent of the stories.[17]

[17] Some earlier research exists on the reporting of benefits and costs associated with specific hazards. Rankin and Nealy (1979), for example, examined the risk/benefit ratio of reporting about coal, nuclear power, and solar energy on network television news, and Nealy, Rankin, and Montano (1978) examined reporting about coal and nuclear

In 1984, hazard stories gave a somewhat greater proportion of space to benefits than they had in 1960. Among energy hazards, the proportion of stories giving at least equal space to benefits was still very small—6.7 percent. In a way, that makes sense. Some energy hazards (e.g., house fires) ordinarily have no benefits. And for others (cars, planes, trains) the benefits may seem so obvious as to require little or no comment. But among stories involving materials hazards and complex technologies, 25.4 percent gave an equal or greater proportion of their space to the benefits of the hazard.

The relative proportions of each hazard story devoted to harms, on the one hand, and benefits, on the other, are an implicit indicator of the cost-benefit ratio (though as we have seen, it may be a misleading one). But it is also possible to mention that ratio *explicitly*, and to indicate whether, in the judgment of the journalist or the source being quoted, costs or benefits predominate in the case of a particular hazard.

In our study relatively few stories—only 8 out of 84, or 9.5 percent in 1960, and 66 out of 410, or 16.1 percent in 1984— explicitly mentioned the ratio of benefits to costs. But where the ratio was mentioned, benefits were said to outweigh costs 75 percent of the time in 1960 and 43.9 percent of the time in 1984. (In about one third of the 1984 stories the ratio was indeterminate.) In other words, when, as in the vast majority of stories, the ratio of benefit to cost was *implicit*, costs clearly appeared to outweigh benefits. But this was not the case when the ratio was explicitly mentioned. Then, when the ratio was clearcut, the benefits of a hazard were said to outweigh its costs.

What was the nature of the stories that gave fairly substantial attention to hazard benefits? Several were stories about exercise or contact sports, but in fact most such stories gave more space to harms than to benefits.[18] One was a story about mushroom

---

power in print media. (The print media were *Time, Business Week, Scientific American, Environment*, the *New York Times, National Observer, Seattle Intelligencer*, and *Chicago Tribune*.) They found that, on television, discussion of benefits outweighed the discussion of costs for solar power, whereas for coal and nuclear power, the proportions were reversed. In print, the discussion of costs outweighed the discussion of benefits in stories about nuclear power and coal.

[18]This was of course true almost by definition, since we did not include in the sample ordinary stories about sports found on the sports pages.

picking. One was a story about aspartame, the only story about this artificial sweetener in our sample. One was a story about drug side effects—but four of five such stories gave more space to the associated risks. Several of the stories we coded about methyl isocyanate gave more space to the pesticide's benefits, or to the economic benefits for the community where it was produced, than to its costs, though the vast majority either gave more emphasis or gave exclusive emphasis to costs.

But by far the largest proportion of hazard stories giving more space to benefits than to costs involved what we called complex technologies. Of the ten complex technologies referred to by the media in 1984, seven produced at least some stories in which the proportion of space devoted to benefits exceeded that devoted to risks. Those seven are shown in Table 5.3, in order of increasing proportion of space devoted to benefits.

For some of these seven, coverage appears to have undergone little change over time (see Pfund and Hofstadter, 1980). For example, two "organ transplant" events were front-page news during our 1984 monitoring period: the baboon heart implanted in "Baby Fae" on October 26, and the artificial heart implanted in William Schroeder on November 25. Almost half of the stories covering these two events discussed no risk issues at all. Of the 37 that did, half devoted more space to the potential dangers of the procedure; the remainder were almost equally divided between emphasizing benefits and giving equal space to both (Table 5.3). But the dangers examined in most of these stories were short-term risks to the specific people involved—risks of organ rejection for Baby Fae, and of blood clotting and stroke for William Schroeder. Only three of the many stories about the artificial heart program examined such issues as the economic costs and the physical and economic costs of alternative treatments. This distribution seems very similar to that described by Pfund and Hofstadter (1981) for the early years of the artificial heart program. News stories about the other kinds of surgery were much more optimistic, as measured by their allocation of space to costs and benefits, than stories about organ transplants. Half of all surgery stories allocated more of their space to benefits than to costs (Table 5.3). Almost all of them were about new surgical procedures or improvements in established procedures. Only one story, about

TABLE 5.3 / **Proportion of Complex Technology Stories Devoting Varying Amounts of Space to Benefits and Costs (1984 Only)**

Complex Technology	More Space to Benefits (%)	Equal Space to Benefits and Costs (%)	More Space to Costs (%)	(N)
Medical care	7.7	7.7	84.6	(13)
Abortion	12.5	12.5	75.0	(8)
Organ transplant	21.6	27.0	51.4	(37)
Recombinant DNA research	33.3	33.3	33.3	(6)
Euthanasia	40.0	33.3	26.7	(15)
Surgery	45.5	27.3	27.3	(11)
Gene therapy	100.0	0.0	0.0	(1)
Bottle feeding	0.0	100.0	0.0	(1)
Medical devices	0.0	0.0	100.0	(1)
Transfusion medicine	0.0	0.0	100.0	(1)

Caesarean section, pointed out the growing and, in its view, excessive use of an old procedure.

In contrast to news coverage of organ transplants, where the emphasis seems to have undergone little change over time, significant changes appear to have taken place in reporting on another complex technology: recombinant DNA (deoxyribonucleic acid) research. In their analysis of the content of coverage on recombinant DNA, Pfund and Hofstadter (1981:143) note that between 1976 and 1979 the emphasis of news stories shifted from risks to benefits, a shift that relegated questions of safety to second place.

In our own research, one third of the stories on recombinant DNA ($N = 6$) gave more space to costs than to benefits, one third gave more to benefits, and one third gave equal space to both. Several of the stories were routine reports of interim rules announced by the EPA for pesticides developed from genetically altered microbes. These gave very little space to either benefits or costs. But two long stories, one in the *Wall Street Journal*, the other in the *New York Times*, both exemplify some of the points made by Pfund and Hofstadter. The *Times* story, by Harold M. Schmeck,

Jr. (October 31, 1984, p. C1), reports on the unanimous decision by the chief federal panel on recombinant DNA research to reject a proposal for banning all gene transplantation from one mammalian species to another and emphasizes the potential benefits of gene transplants in treating diseases and developing new food sources. Although it presents the positions of Jeremy Rifkin and Michael Fox, both of whom oppose the technology, it devotes much more space to refuting those positions, especially Rifkin's.

The long *Journal* article, by Patricia A. Bellew (Nov. 21, 1984, p. 1), attends to both the risks and the benefits of genetic engineering in agricultural research. However, by its sequence of quotations, it manages to deprecate critics of the technology, especially Rifkin. "'Who knows whether those microbes are going to migrate and create havoc?'" Rifkin is quoted as asking. "'Once these bacteria get out, you can't put them back in a drum.'" And then comes the response: "Scientists working with the ice-minus bug [a genetically altered microbe designed to keep frost from forming on plants] scoff at their fears. . . . 'This whole controversy is bloody absurd,'" John Bedbrook, the scientific director of Advanced Genetic Sciences, Inc., a company planning to test the microbe, is quoted as saying.[19]

Another hazard whose coverage exemplifies dramatic change over time is abortion. Six of the eight news stories about abortion[20] that appeared in the press in 1984 devoted more space to harms than to benefits. But in 1984 the harms discussed were always those to the fetus. None of the stories mentioned the risks posed to the mother by illegal abortions in the years prior to the 1973 U.S. Supreme Court ruling striking down state abortion laws, and virtually none mentioned any benefits of abortion. We found no news stories about abortion in the media we monitored during 1960. But just before our sampling period began, on August 15, 1960, *Newsweek* carried a long story (pp. 50–52) about abortion that made no mention of harms to the fetus but, instead, empha-

---

[19] Nevertheless, Slovic (1987:285) cautions that DNA technologies seem to evoke several of the same risk perceptions as nuclear energy. As a result, he points out, "this technology could face some of the same problems and opposition now confronting the nuclear industry," especially in the event of an accident.

[20] We did not include in our sample news stories dealing with political issues only (e.g., the position taken by a candidate for office in the 1984 election).

sized the risks to women undergoing illegal abortions. Similarly, a scanning of articles on abortion that appeared in *Time* and *Newsweek* during 1969 turned up many references to the mother's plight, but little, if any, attention to that of the fetus. However, as legal rulings have increasingly narrowed the scope of *Roe* v. *Wade* and generated increased activism by proponents of abortion, there is some indication that news coverage may again be inclining toward an emphasis on the potential risks of such restrictions to the mother.

Unlike the coverage of abortion, coverage of another complex technology, euthanasia,[21] tended in 1984 to emphasize benefits rather than costs (Table 5.3). (We found no stories at all about euthanasia in 1960.) The stories in which euthanasia was discussed varied. Both the *Times* and an ABC newscast on September 21, 1984, for example, covered a news conference by five French doctors who said they had helped some of their patients to die. The press conference was held on the eve of a conference on the "Right to Die with Dignity." Although coverage of the conference could have provided a forum for discussing the risks to patients posed by delegating such decisions to doctors and others, these issues were not raised. Instead, the focus of the news stories was on benefits to patients and on the legal risks run by the doctors.

True, several stories on the Reagan administration's "Baby Doe" rules, intended to permit prosecution of medical personnel who did not treat severely handicapped infants, emphasized the risk to the infants of withholding such treatment. But stories involving euthanasia for elderly or disabled patients tended instead to emphasize benefits for the patients or their kin. Only one story (NBC, Sept. 8, 1984), about a lawsuit against New York Hospital for failing to rescuscitate an elderly patient, explicitly raised the issue of costs and accountability by citing unnamed "state officials": "Without government safeguards to assure that resuscitation decisions are not made carelessly, unilaterally, or anonymously, the potential for abuse is present in every hospital in this country."

Over the past few years the subject of euthanasia has received

---

[21] By euthanasia, we mean to include active as well as passive ways of facilitating the death of another person for reasons of mercy.

increasing attention and debate in the mass media. Indeed, the issue has reached so widely into the public arena that, in the state of Washington in the fall of 1991, a right-to-die referendum was presented to the voters. Though the referendum was defeated, 47 percent of the voters voted for it, and it is our impression that media coverage in recent years has become much more balanced in its coverage of the benefits and costs of euthanasia decisions. Several different events, dramatizing the issue, have triggered widespread media attention: the drawn-out vigil and legal battle of the parents of the vegetatively comatose Nancy Kruzan; the "mercy" killing, by Rudolfo Linares, of his partially brain-dead ten-month-old son by disconnecting his life-support system; the emergence of Dr. Jack Kevorkian, media-labeled as the "suicide doctor" or "Dr. Death"; and the medical-journal confession of Dr. Timothy Quill of his decision to willingly assist in a dying patient's suicide.

Thus, reporting on recombinant DNA, abortion, and euthanasia vividly exemplifies one aspect of what we refer to as changing definitions of risk, whether initiated by the media or not. Although we can illustrate these changing definitions, we cannot so easily answer questions about what determines them. It is our impression that the mass media we monitored rarely structured the terms of the debate with respect to any of these hazards.[22] Rather, they tended to accept the frames provided by the dominant institutions currently active in the debate. For example, in 1984 the initiative on abortion was being taken by the Catholic church and by right-to-life groups trying to change the current legal status of abortion in the United States. The terms of the debate, as framed by these organizations, emphasized the harms done to the fetus, and the media covered these organizations and framed the issues in their terms. Earlier, the proabortion forces were the ones trying to change the status quo; and when the media covered their activities, it covered the issues they raised, instead.

Social and intellectual currents seem to obey Hegelian laws of

[22] One way in which the media, especially magazines, have structured the debate with respect to tobacco (and, inferentially, other hazards) is by ignoring and even suppressing information about its harmful effects. See Weis and Burke (1987); Kessler (1989); Warner and others (1992).

thesis and antithesis, action and reaction. In the broadest sense, this means swings of optimism and pessimism in the perspective on human affairs. For example, in the United States, the period from the mid-thirties to about 1970 coupled an emphasis on environmental determinants of personality, intelligence, health, and behavior with an optimistic conviction that all of these were malleable and meliorable. Since the early seventies, these emphases have gradually given way to explanations emphasizing biological and hereditary factors, and a concomitant belief that much of human nature and behavior is predetermined and, for better or worse, fixed.[23] But this is not the first repetition of the cycle (previous examples include nineteenth-century biological explanations of criminality, such as those of Lombroso and Gall, and, more generally, nineteenth-century reactions to the social implications of Darwin's theory of evolution), nor is it likely to be the last. However, as molecular biologists have begun to make progress in identifying and even correcting genetic defects, it is possible that what has previously been associated with a pessimistic and deterministic view of the human condition may come to be perceived as optimistic and melioristic, instead.

On a smaller scale, we can observe cyclical swings in emphasis on nuclear power benefits ("then") and costs ("now"), on legal abortion benefits ("then") and costs ("now"), on recombinant DNA risks ("then") and benefits ("now"), on euthanasia benefits ("now") and risks (when?). "Then" and "now" are deliberately vague, as are estimates of trends. But, for example, in our data the cost-benefit ratio of nuclear power stories changed from five out of eleven that mentioned only benefits and three of eleven that gave more space to costs in 1960, to one of nine that mentioned only benefits and six of nine that gave a greater proportion of space to cost in 1984. And while recombinant DNA technology may have gotten more favorable treatment in the eighties than in the seventies for many reasons, one of those reasons, we believe, is society's increasing infatuation with biological determinants in general. The media do not initiate these cycles, they only reflect and amplify them.

[23] E.g., "Kinsey Study Finds Homosexuals Show Early Predisposition (*New York Times*, Aug. 23, 1981); "Major Personality Study Finds That Traits Are Mostly Inherited" (*New York Times*, Dec. 2, 1986); "New Focus on Chemistry of Anhedonia" (*New York Times*, Mar. 15, 1983).

Who Benefits?

As part of our examination of media definitions of hazard benefits and costs, we coded the recipient of the benefits for each story
that mentioned them at all. When benefits were mentioned—and
that, it will be remembered, was in a minority of stories—overwhelmingly, victims were included among the beneficiaries. This
was true 100 percent and 75 percent of the time, respectively, for
energy and materials hazards in 1960; and 91 percent and 75 percent of the time in 1984. And more often than not, it was the
victim only who was said to benefit, rather than the victim and
someone else.

In part, this finding follows from our analysis of the hazards
for which benefits were most likely to be mentioned (i.e., complex
technologies such as organ transplants, other kinds of surgery,
and euthanasia, from which victims do stand to benefit). But
though there are potential beneficiaries of these procedures other
than the victims (e.g, the doctors developing the techniques and
the medical institutions where they are being done), these are
mentioned less often. In 1984, "other" beneficiaries were mentioned together with victims 27.6 percent of the time, and "other"
beneficiaries only, 25.2 percent of the time.

HAZARD ALTERNATIVES

Besides looking at benefits mentioned in connection with a
given hazard, we also looked at whether or not the story mentioned any alternatives to the hazard. In 1960 only about 13 percent of the stories made reference to some alternative (either
another hazard or, perhaps, no action); but by 1984, some 27.7
percent of stories contained such a reference. Like the mention of
benefits, these references were almost twice as likely to occur in
stories involving materials hazards and complex technologies as
in stories about energy hazards or activities entailing benefits and
costs.

And although the 1960 news stories we analyzed overwhelmingly indicated a preference for the alternative hazard, in 1984 this
was no longer so clear, especially in the case of materials hazards
and complex technologies. In 1960, four out of five stories indi-

implied ratio, based on the relative space given to harms and to benefits, was heavily weighted on the side of harm. The press depicts specific incidents with a fair amount of accuracy. But it does not ordinarily go beyond the specific incident to explore more general issues of cost and benefit, risk and gain.

The question has been raised as to whether the media's preoccupation with bad news contributed to what some writers (e.g., Wildavsky) have termed increasing "risk-averseness" on the part of the American public.[24] That question would probably have to be answered in the negative. Newspaper and newsmagazine reporting about risks has not become less precise in the last twenty-five years, nor has it become more heavily oriented toward harms. Nor is it likely, though we have not performed the quantitative analysis, that the press of a still earlier era was any less attentive to disaster. So changes in public fearfulness, if they exist, cannot be attributed to changes in reporting practices in the print media. It is possible that the vividness of hazard reporting on television, a relatively recent phenomenon, may contribute to such a result, but the data available from the present study do not permit us to answer that question.

[24] Wildavsky writes: "How extraordinary! The richest, longest lived, best protected, most resourceful civilization, with the highest degree of insight into its own technology, is on its way to becoming the most frightened. Is it our environment or ourselves that have changed? Would people like us have had this sort of concern in the past?"—quoted in Slovic (1987:236). And though there is no evidence that the media portray more hazards now than they did in 1960, a 1980 poll by Louis Harris and Associates indicates that approximately 80 percent of Americans agree that "people are subject to more risk today than they were 20 years ago." See Johnson and Covello (1987: p. vii).

6 / Blame

What does it mean to assign blame? Philosophers and psychologists have tried to understand and explain the complex assumptions and processes entailed in ordinary attributions of blame.[1] Cultural anthropologists have tried to discern the role of culture in determining which hazards we attend to and how we ascribe responsibility for them (see Douglas and Wildavsky, 1982; Jasanoff, 1986). Sociologists such as Nelkin see social and political conditions as decisive: "Concern about risk may depend less on the nature of the danger than on the observers' political and cultural biases. It is the social system, the world view, the ideological premises of a group or a society that shapes perception of risk" (Nelkin 1985a:16; see also Nelkin, 1988). And as if in unconscious echo, the *Wall Street Journal*, in an editorial on a liquefied natural

---

[1]For an extensive exploration along these lines, see Shaver (1985). A more recent treatment, relating more directly to blame and risk, is presented by Tennen and Affleck (1990:209) in their article, "Blaming Others for Threatening Events," in which they review 25 published studies that have reported, usually as an incidental finding, the adaptational impact of blaming others for threatening events. Others, for example legal scholars, have examined more specialized forms of assigning blame.

gas (LNG) explosion in Mexico City fatal to more than 300 people, contrasts the absence of "hysteria" about the dangers of storing and transporting liquefied natural gas with the "uproar" following the accident at the Three Mile Island nuclear power facility. The *Journal* notes, "Obviously, there is much more to the anti-nuclear movement than mere considerations of safety" (Nov. 23, 1984, p. 6).

In our society, it may seem only natural to blame irresponsible drinkers for alcohol-related vehicular accidents, and to blame industry for "industrial waste" hazards. But Gusfield (1981), along with Douglas and Wildavsky, and Nelkin, reminds us of the cultural and social bases of our conception of reality, and emphasizes that our understandings and diagnoses are only "natural," "inevitable," and "indisputable" within a particular sociocultural framework. How public attention and concern are channeled toward particular dangers, how those dangers are defined, and how responsibility for them is affixed all reflect social processes, not absolute, inevitable conditions.

Although there may be strenuous arguments over which individuals or groups are most to blame for some hazard or disaster, those arguments (the terms of the debate, the nature of the evidence marshaled by each side) are framed by shared sociocultural assumptions. These assumptions are usually so taken for granted that they not only seem beyond debate, but are invisible to all but the most trained eye. Arguments proceed within the confines of dominant paradigms, which impose limits on the extent of disagreement even as they facilitate debate on its finer points.

And not just who is blamed or held accountable, but even the inclination to ascribe blame at all, may differ from one culture to another. In a society like ours, the need to fix responsibility, to locate a cause and preferably an agent, is pervasive. "How did you catch that cold?" is a question parents commonly put to their children, hoping to find a chain of interruptible events even at the risk of evoking unwarranted feelings of guilt. In such a culture the ultimate horror is a disaster without an explanation, an essentially random event. When, for example, an Aeromexico DC-9 jetliner smashed into a group of homes in a residential area in Cerritos, California, on September 1, 1986, killing some members of families but sparing others in essentially accidental patterns, the *New York Times* headlined its news story, "Randomness of Disaster Leaves Area in Shock" (September 2, 1986). Not only the disaster itself but its senselessness and unpredictability were what residents found particularly disturbing.

In our own study of hazard reporting, we assumed that the media would reflect some shared beliefs about responsibility, danger, and risk as well as potentially influencing them. In order to illuminate these beliefs, we approached questions of accountability and blame by introducing a comparative frame of reference whenever possible. In the first place, we hypothesized that different categories of hazard would elicit different patterns of blaming. Second, we tried to distinguish between responsibility (blameworthiness) for a hazard and responsibility for taking precautions against it. Third, we examined these patterns in different media and in different years. Finally, we examined certain concepts related to responsibility and blame: regulation, litigation, and cost. And we examined whether exposure to the hazard was voluntary or not.

PATTERNS OF BLAMING

Related Research

At the outset, we should note some convergences between our work and that of other researchers. In a fascinating series of studies on what they call "attitudes of social justice," Piazza and his colleagues set out to measure people's explanations for various social problems (see Apostle, Glock, Piazza, and Suelzle, 1983; Glock and Piazza, 1981). For example, they may tell respondents that blacks, on average, are not as well off as whites in America, and ask whether this situation arises because of social conditions, because blacks do not try hard enough, because God made the races different, or because of some other specific reasons.

These "explanatory modes," as Piazza and his colleagues call them, have proved to be good predictors of policy positions in several substantive areas, and are thus useful for monitoring socially significant changes in attitudes over time. Based on preliminary research, Piazza and his colleagues note that most explanations of racial inequalities in living standards can be grouped into the following categories: God; genetic factors; cultural factors; individual efforts; overt discrimination; and social conditions, with individual efforts and social conditions being mentioned most frequently.

Another research program with marked resemblances to ours is that of Iyengar (1987), who has been looking at how such issues as poverty and unemployment are framed in television news and how such framing, in turn, influences viewers' perceptions of who is to blame for various events and problems and who is responsible for their resolution or prevention. Iyengar distinguishes between "episodic" and "thematic" framing of issues—a distinction corresponding to the one we make between "event-only" and "issue-oriented" hazard stories (see Chapter 3).[2] As predicted, subjects exposed to specially constructed videotapes in which an experimental news story was embedded tended to attribute responsibility to individuals when the story was episodic, and to societal institutions when the story was thematic. Iyengar believes that television's predominantly episodic treatment of the news inhibits attribution of responsibility to politicians or political institutions.

Blame and Responsibility for Hazards

On the basis of pretesting, we developed the following list of blameworthy agents who frequently appeared in media accounts of hazards: victims; other individuals; social categories (e.g., women and blacks); business or industry; doctors or medicine; government; and God or nature. More than one of these could be coded for each media account, but the coder was asked to indicate, if possible, which of them was "the most important" agent of blame.

We also developed a number of common-sense expectations about likely targets of blame in our society for different categories of hazard. The test of these hypotheses is based on the "most important" target of blame in each story.[3]

---

[2]Because, in our study, event-only stories were not coded in the same detail as issue stories, we cannot replicate Iyengar's analysis with our data.

[3]Although as many as eight distinct targets of blame could be coded for any one article, over 80 percent specified only one. Of those that mentioned more than one, almost 80 percent listed only two, and the remaining 23 percent never listed more than three.

1. We expected that stories about "natural hazards" would, almost by definition, tend to blame God or nature, even though in some cases—for example, floods or mudslides exacerbated by deforestation, or famines made worse by inequities of distribution—human beings clearly played a role.

2. We expected stories about activities involving benefits and costs to blame the victims, largely because most such activities entail voluntary, indeed voluntary and deliberate, exposure to the hazard. Barton (1969) had speculated that where there are vested interests in the causes of disasters, mass media content would blame the victim. We, in turn, hypothesized that where there are vested interests in risk factors (e.g., cigarettes and alcohol), the media would emphasize modes of risk reduction that place the burden of control on the individual rather than on regulation of the industry involved.

3. Stories about energy hazards are often stories about a diverse category of "accidents." We expected a sizable fraction of these to blame the victim (for example, for not wearing a seat belt), but, especially after 1960, we expected a certain proportion to blame business or industry as well.

4. We expected that stories about materials hazards would, at least in 1984, emphasize the culpability of business or industry. This assumption is based on precedent—for example, highly dramatic reporting of industrial accidents such as Three Mile Island and of industrial waste "time bombs" such as Love Canal in New York State, or Times Beach, Missouri, as well as highly publicized exposés of industrial disregard for safety going back to Ralph Nader's *Unsafe at Any Speed* or Rachel Carson's *Silent Spring*.

5. Stories about complex technology, which in our definition involved predominantly medical technology, would, we expected, most often blame doctors or medicine.

6. Finally, we expected that stories about illness would tend either to blame God/nature or the victim. The tendency to blame the victim would, we thought, be greater in 1984 than in 1960 because of the increased emphasis on individual competence and responsibility for personal health.[4]

[4]Nelkin (1988:371) notes: "In the contemporary American context, the rhetoric of blame has been most evident in the discourse on preventive medicine and its emphasis on individual responsibility. In 1979, a surgeon general's report called *Healthy People* concluded that the foremost causes of illness lie in individual behavior. Hailed in the press as the manifesto of a public-health revolution, the report urged extensive changes in lifestyle as the way to avoid disease. Subsequently a series of government reports on chronic diseases has attributed disease to problematic individual behavior: to smoking, dietary habits, or personal excess."

TABLE 6.1 / **Percentage of Stories Indicating Blame, by Hazard and Year**

Hazard Category	1960 (%)	1960 (N)	1984 (%)	1984 (N)
		Year		
Natural hazards	71.4	(28)	67.6	(102)
Activities with B/C	25.0	(4)	58.1	(43)
Energy hazards	55.1	(49)	54.3	(92)
Materials hazards	37.5	(24)	76.5	(179)
Complex technologies	83.3	(12)	75.5	(98)
Illnesses	17.5	(40)	12.1	(110)
TOTAL	47.1	(157)	58.5	(624)
	$\chi^2 = 47.0$;		$\chi^2 = 277.0$;	
	$df = 5; p < .01$		$df = 5; p < .01$	

To begin with, we should note that the tendency to attribute blame was not universal. In 1984, 35.6 percent of the stories analyzed in detail (i.e., not "event-only" stories) made no explicit or implicit mention of blame at all, and in 1960 the percentage was higher still (45 percent).

As can be seen from Table 6.1, the tendency to assign blame or responsibility was not constant across hazard categories, though with the exception of materials hazards and hazards involving benefits and costs, there was virtually no change between 1960 and 1984. In both years, most stories about natural hazards and complex technologies ascribed responsibility for the hazard, as did about half of the energy hazard stories. But less than 20 percent of illness stories attributed responsibility for the illness to anyone or anything.

This finding seems to challenge our earlier generalization about the United States as a blaming society. However, in some of these stories, the absence of an explicit or implicit attribution of blame may reflect the fact that responsibility for the hazard is assumed to be so obvious that no attribution is required, as in the roughly 30 percent of natural hazard stories coded as containing no attribution of blame. In others, it is clear that responsibility attaches to prevention of the hazard, and it is this responsibility that the news account features, either explicitly or implicitly. Between 72 percent

TABLE 6.2 / Percentage of Stories Indicating Responsibility for Prevention, by Hazard and Year

Hazard Category	1960 (%)	(N)	1984 (%)	(N)
Natural hazards	71.4	(28)	71.6	(102)
Activities with B/C	75.0	(4)	79.1	(43)
Energy hazards	61.2	(49)	82.6	(92)
Materials hazards	75.0	(24)	81.0	(179)
Complex technologies	58.3	(12)	84.7	(98)
Illnesses	45.0	(40)	46.4	(110)
TOTAL	61.1	(157)	74.0	(624)
	$\chi^2 = 8.57$; $df = 5$; ns		$\chi^2 = 53.0$; $df = 5$; $p < .01$	

and 85 percent of all news accounts except those involving illness made some attribution of responsibility for prevention in 1984 (see Table 6.2).

The big change between 1960 and 1984, a doubling in the tendency to ascribe blame, comes in the categories of materials hazards and hazards involving benefits and costs. In both cases, the change is due less to a change in the tendency to attribute blame for those hazards mentioned in 1960 than it is to the emergence of many different hazards in 1984. However, the change is not attributable to the heavy coverage of MIC in 1984. The tendency to attribute blame is not much higher in MIC stories (79.3 percent) than it is in stories about other materials hazards in 1984 (74.2 percent).

Of those news stories in 1984 that did assign blame, roughly one quarter mentioned more than one source; 41 percent of these multiples could not be coded for a main source. Thus, in 1984, we had 359 stories out of 624, or 57.5 percent, that blamed someone or something and for which we were able to code the main source of blame. In 1960, 64 of 157 stories, or 40.8 percent, were available for such analysis.

When we examined the pattern of blaming in these stories, most of our expectations appear to be confirmed (see Table 6.3).

TABLE 6.3 / Percentage of Stories Indicating Target of Blame, by Hazard Category and Year

Hazard Category	Victim (%)	Other Individual (%)	Business, Industry (%)	Doctors, Medicine (%)	Gov't (%)	God, Nature (%)	Other (%)	(N)
				1960				
Natural	5.3	0.0	5.3	5.3	5.3	73.7	5.3	(19)
B/C	100.0	0.0	0.0	0.0	0.0	0.0	0.0	(1)
Energy	11.5	15.4	3.8	0.0	23.1	11.5	34.6	(26)
Materials	11.1	0.0	55.6	0.0	22.2	0.0	11.1	(9)
Complex	0.0	10.0	10.0	30.0	0.0	0.0	50.0	(10)
Illness	14.3	14.3	28.6	14.3	0.0	14.3	14.3	(7)
TOTAL	9.7	8.3	13.9	6.9	12.5	25.0	23.6	(72)
	%	%	%	1984 %	%	%	%	(N)
Natural	4.5	0.0	0.0	0.0	20.9	70.1	4.5	(67)
B/C	62.5	16.7	4.2	0.0	4.2	4.2	8.4	(24)
Energy	10.2	2.0	40.8	0.0	24.5	6.1	16.3	(49)
Materials	15.6	5.2	72.6	1.5	5.2	0.0	0.0	(135)
Complex	4.1	12.3	8.2	70.0	2.7	1.4	1.4	(73)
Illness	45.5	27.3	0.0	0.0	9.1	18.2	0.0	(11)
TOTAL	14.5	6.7	34.8	14.8	10.3	15.0	3.9	(359)

Target of Blame

However, cell sizes are too small to permit reliable comparisons, and therefore no significance tests have been computed.

1. In 70 percent of the 67 stories about natural hazards that assigned any blame in 1984, God or nature was the most important target of blame; the same was true of 74 percent of 19 stories in 1960. Government was seen as responsible in 21 percent of the remaining stories in 1984, but only 5 percent in 1960.

    An example of a story blaming nature for the Ethiopian famine is one in the *New York Times* (Sept. 29, 1984, p. 5): "Ethiopia is facing a disastrous drought which is worse than the great drought of the early seventies. In 1974, 200,000 Ethiopians starved to death. . . . This time at least 6 million people are at risk *owing to the failure of the belg, or light rains.*" (The phrase on which the coding is based has been italicized.)

    Predominantly, news accounts of natural disasters such as famine tell simple stories in which starvation is the result of scarcity, which in turn is attributable to natural forces. Only a small minority elaborate these accounts to introduce explanations such as political power as factors in the disaster.[5]

2. Sixty-three percent of 24 stories about hazards involving benefits and costs blamed the victim in 1984, with the only other category receiving more than 8 percent of mentions being "other individuals." There was only one benefit-cost story that assigned blame in 1960. Thus, the kinds of hazards we have classified as "activities involving benefits and costs" were primarily perceived as entailing individual responsibility. Furthermore, when we looked specifically at alcohol and tobacco use, we found, as expected, that all stories involving alcohol attributed blame to someone or something, as did 11 out of 12 stories about tobacco. (Only one story about either of these hazards was available for analysis in 1960.) In 72.7 percent of 11 stories involving tobacco use, the victim was blamed for ill effects; the same was true in only 38.5 percent of 13 stories involving the effects of alcohol. This last is still a substantially higher proportion than for other materials hazards, though it is lower than for other activities involving benefits and costs.

    In one story involving alcohol as a hazard, for example, the drunk driver was held accountable not only morally but also legally for the resulting accident: " 'Drunk driving is a serious

---

[5]Desai (1987:398) has pointed out that most economists similarly ignore noneconomic forces; and he argues for a reconsideration of this practice: "Thus, while most economists tell stories, these stories have real consequences. It is necessary to examine them not only for their appeal and elegance . . . but also for the real life policy choices they entail."

threat to everyone,' said Brooklyn District Attorney Elizabeth Holtzman. 'Drunk drivers in Brooklyn must get the message that if a car in their hands becomes a vehicle for injury or death, it will be taken from them.' " The driver was also sentenced to "mandatory participation in an alcoholic treatment program" (*Amsterdam News*, Dec. 29, 1984, p. 9). Most of the news stories about tobacco focused on efforts to get smokers to stop. Such stories were coded as holding the victim responsible for tobacco's ill effects as well as for their prevention. In contrast to other materials hazards, business or industry was blamed in only 16.7 percent of these 24 stories about alcohol or tobacco; most of the remainder blamed "other individuals."

Because tobacco and alcohol had been classified as materials hazards by Hohenemser et al. (1983), we classified them that way as well. However, as "drinking" and "smoking," they might equally well have been classified as "activities involving benefits and costs," and the pattern of blaming associated with them conforms much more closely to that for benefit-cost activities than to that for materials hazards. The implication, especially in news stories about smoking, is that these hazards are a matter of individual choice and, therefore, of individual responsibility.

3. We had no clearcut anticipations concerning the attribution of blame in stories about energy hazards, though we expected some attribution to victims and, especially after 1960, to industry. In fact, only 10 percent of such stories in 1984 blamed the victim or another individual (e.g., stories like the CBS report of an AMTRAK collision [Oct. 17, 1984], which concluded: "A spokesman said the signal system seemed to be working normally and that human error appeared involved in the collision"); 41 percent blamed industry (e.g., "Clipped Wings— Safety Lapses Ground an Airline," *Time*, Nov. 26, 1984, p. 85, which reported: "The [Federal Aviation Adminstration] said that [Provincetown-Boston Airline] was guilty of potentially dangerous cost-cutting practices"); and 25 percent blamed government, with the rest scattered among other categories. Most of the 1984 energy hazard stories in which government was held to be responsible involved stories about nuclear arms. In 1960, by way of contrast and as we predicted, only 4 percent of the stories blamed industry, the percentages blaming victims and government remaining largely unchanged.

Unlike stories about alcohol and tobacco, most stories about automobile crashes (10 out of 12 in 1984 and 6 out of 7 in 1960) did not address the issue of blame at all. The small minority that did tended to blame the victim. In both 1960 and 1984 almost half of all energy stories failed to address the issue of blame. In a sense, the implication of such an omission is that no one was to blame, or conversely, that a consensus about blame makes a specific reference unnecessary.[6]

4. As we have indicated, we expected stories about materials hazards to emphasize the responsibility of business and industry, especially in 1984. And indeed, 73 percent of 135 stories about materials hazards that assigned any blame attributed that blame to business/industry. In an additional 5 percent of stories, the government was assigned blame; the victim was blamed in only 16 percent of stories about materials hazards.

   However, the heavy concentration of blame on industry in 1984 is largely attributable to the oversampling of MIC stories, 97 percent of which attributed responsibility for the disaster to Union Carbide. In the remaining materials hazards stories the proportion blaming industry was 49 percent, in fact a little lower than the 56 percent figure for 1960.

5. As we expected, in 1984 most (70 percent of 73) stories about what we called complex technologies held doctors or medicine responsible for risks associated with the hazard; the rest scattered responsibility among other sources. In 1960, only 30 percent of complex technology stories blamed doctors or medicine, with 50 percent blaming "other" sources, primarily governments other than that of the United States. However, this change in emphasis is attributable to different hazards being featured in the two years rather than to any change in the tendency to blame a particular source for a particular hazard. In 1960, 8 of the 10 complex technology stories were about inadequate medical care, often in Third World countries. In 1984, stories about organ transplants were much more numerous in this category.

6. Contrary to our expectations, the overall tendency to ascribe any blame or responsibility for illness was no greater in 1984 than it had been in 1960, and was slight in both years: 12 percent in 1984, vs. 18 percent in 1960 (see Table 6.1). The tendency was, however, greater in stories about AIDS than in stories about other illnesses: 24 percent of AIDS stories, compared with 12 percent of illness stories in general, assigned blame or responsibility; and all of those that did blamed either the victim (67 percent) or another individual (33 percent). Putting this an-

---

[6]In addition, as pointed out earlier, responsibility in such stories may be focused on prevention. As with other kinds of hazard stories, the proportion of energy stories attributing responsibility for prevention was considerably higher than the proportion attributing blame (see Tables 6.1 and 6.2).

other way, in 1984 5 out of 12 illness stories assigning any blame at all blamed the victim. Four out of 5 of these were stories about AIDS. Among those statements coded as blaming the victim were references to AIDS being transmitted by sharing contaminated needles for injecting drugs or by engaging in casual sex with multiple partners.[7] In 1960, only 1 out of 7 illness stories assigning any blame at all had blamed the victim.

Thus, there appears to be a difference in blaming between stories about AIDS and stories about other illnesses. However, this conclusion must be tempered by pointing out that we had no comparable mysterious and deadly infectious diseases in our sample, either in 1960 or in 1984.

With respect to infectious diseases and, increasingly, certain kinds of cancers, the issue of responsibility or blame is confused with issues of prevention. Perhaps because AIDS is caused by a virus transmitted by blood or semen, victims are seen as causing their illness by engaging in behavior that transmits it. If, instead, the viruses were airborne, such attributions of blame would presumably be much more difficult to make. And indeed, when the infection is known to have been caused by an involuntary blood transfusion or the use of contaminated clotting factor by hemophiliacs, the tendency to blame the victim is withheld.

The media, of course, do not originate these attitudes of blame.[8] But the attitudes are beginning to be reflected in sexual attitudes and behavior, as reported in surveys of the public. For example, recent surveys have found substantial proportions of the public, especially those who are younger and single, claiming to have changed their sexual behavior in order to avoid exposure to the AIDS virus (Singer, Rogers, and Glassman, 1991). And the General Social Survey has reported small increases over the last several years in the percentage of people believing extramarital sex

---

[7]For example, "Bathhouses and booths in bookstores *allow frequent and often anonymous sexual contact, believed to be a major factor in the spread of the disease*" (CBS, Oct. 9, 1984). "In San Francisco today, the extent of AIDS led public health officials to shut down several bathhouses and bars. These allegedly were *providing places for promiscuous homosexual activity*, which, scientists agree, *is the major cause of the spread of AIDS*" (NBC, Oct. 9, 1984). Phrases on which the coding is based have been italicized.

[8]In fact, as can be seen from the examples cited in the text, it is generally not the reporter but a specific source who is quoted as attributing blame or resonsibility. In their analysis of media effects, Page and Shapiro (1992) distinguish among these sources. We have not attempted to do so.

is wrong (Smith, 1990). Psychologists are beginning to be preoccupied, once again, with sexual guilt, after years in which its presumed absence was the focus of attention (see Goleman, 1985).

In summary, our expectations about varying patterns of blame attribution for different types of hazards were largely supported by the data. But our predictions of changes over time were generally not borne out. Although we might have observed such changes had we selected a longer interval, our study provides no evidence that cultural patterns of attributing blame for specific dangers have undergone any notable change in the past twenty-five years.

RESPONSIBILITY FOR PREVENTION

In analyzing the attribution of responsibility for hazards we tried to separate blame for the hazard itself from responsibility for its prevention. Although it was sometimes difficult to distinguish between the two concepts, prevention was clearly the easier one to identify. In virtually every comparison, both in 1960 and in 1984, a higher proportion of stories identified someone as responsible for preventing a hazard than identified a source of blame for the hazard itself (see Tables 6.1 and 6.2). Nor is there a great deal of variation in this regard among hazards, especially in 1984: with the exception of illness, about four-fifths of stories about all types of hazards in 1984 identified someone as responsible for prevention, and even stories about illness did so almost 50 percent of the time. The proportions are virtually identical for 1960, except that news accounts of energy hazards and complex technologies were less likely to ascribe responsibility for prevention in 1960 than in 1984.

The results of our analysis of media attribution of responsibility for prevention are shown in Table 6.4. Again, as in Table 6.3, cell sizes are too small to permit reliable comparisons. Overall, there was a somewhat greater tendency to assign responsibility for hazard prevention to government in 1960 than in 1984 (46 percent vs. 39 percent of all stories assigned responsibility for prevention to government in those years), and there appears to be a more pronounced tendency to target business and industry for prevention in 1984 than in 1960 (15 percent vs. 4 percent).

TABLE 6.4 / Percentage of Stories Indicating Agent Responsible for Prevention, by Hazard Category and Year

Hazard Category	Agent Responsible for Prevention							
	Victim (%)	Other Individual (%)	Business, Industry (%)	Doctors, Medicine (%)	Gov't (%)	God, Nature (%)	Other (%)	(N)
				1960				
Natural	20.0	10.0	0.0	5.0	40.0	0.0	25.0	(20)
B/C	66.7	33.3	0.0	0.0	0.0	0.0	0.0	(3)
Energy	6.7	3.3	10.0	0.0	73.3	0.0	6.7	(30)
Material	23.5	0.0	5.9	0.0	52.9	0.0	17.6	(17)
Complex	0.0	0.0	0.0	14.3	57.1	0.0	28.6	(7)
Illness	44.4	0.0	0.0	38.9	5.6	0.0	11.1	(18)
TOTAL	21.0	4.2	4.2	9.5	46.3	0.0	14.7	(95)
				1984				
	(%)	(%)	(%)	(%)	(%)	(%)	(%)	(N)
Natural	10.1	0.0	0.0	0.0	30.4	0.0	59.4	(69)
B/C	63.6	3.0	15.2	0.0	18.2	0.0	0.0	(33)
Energy	10.8	9.5	16.2	0.0	60.8	0.0	2.7	(74)
Material	14.5	2.8	33.8	0.0	49.0	0.0	0.0	(145)
Complex	2.4	4.8	2.4	53.0	31.3	0.0	6.0	(83)
Illness	52.9	4.0	2.0	21.6	13.7	0.0	5.9	(51)
TOTAL	18.9	4.0	15.2	12.1	38.7	0.0	11.2	(455)

The shift away from government seems to occur in all hazard categories except that of illness, though in the case of natural hazards, materials hazards, and complex technologies the reasons may have more to do with the mix of specific hazards than with any general trend. For example, stories about the Ethiopian famine dominated the natural hazards category in 1984, and "other governments" (coded as "other") were more often held responsible for preventing the consequences of famine than the Ethiopian government itself. Similarly, perhaps because of the heavy attention to two organ transplant cases in the news in 1984, doctors were more often targeted for preventive responsibility than government. Of course, this need not have been the case. For example, news stories might have focused on government regulation of the procedure, rather than on the efforts of individual surgeons. In the case of materials hazards, 70.9 percent of stories attributing responsibility for preventing the risks associated with MIC named industry, whereas 61.1 percent of all other stories in this category named government. Thus, the apparently increasing trend to hold industry responsible for preventing materials hazards is in fact attributable to the oversampling of MIC stories alone.

As we have seen, stories about alcohol and tobacco disproportionately blamed victims for risks associated with these hazards. In the case of tobacco, victims also appear to be disproportionately held responsible for prevention: 66.7 percent of the time, compared with 25 percent for industry and 8.5 percent for government. In the case of alcohol, however, it was government that appears to be seen as primarily responsible for prevention, with victims and other individuals each held accountable 25 percent of the time. In no story was the liquor industry implicated in prevention. Thus, judging from the evidence of these stories, smoking was seen primarily as an activity within the individual's control, whereas prevention of the risks of drinking was seen, in the majority of stories, as requiring government intervention through the imposition of laws and the like.

Although, as we have noted, it was sometimes difficult to distinguish between blame and responsibility for prevention, these are in fact two distinct concepts, as is evident from their different patterns of attribution. Overwhelmingly, for example, nature or God appears to be blamed for the occurrence of natural hazards, but governments are responsible for preventing them, or the damage caused by them. Industry appears to be blamed most often for materials hazards but government is primarily responsible for preventing them. And while government and, especially, industry appear to be seen as responsible for energy hazards in 1984, it was principally government that was seen as responsible for their prevention. Only in the case of illnesses and hazards involving benefits and costs did blame and responsibility for prevention appear to be overwhelmingly located in the same agent—i.e., the victim. However, as can be seen from Tables 6.1 and 6.2, many more stories assigned responsibility for illness prevention than attributed blame for the illness itself—in 1984, almost four times as many. A similar, less striking trend was evident in the case of benefit-cost stories.

When news stories target agents of responsibility, whether for blame or prevention, those citations can be deliberate and explicit, or else subtle and implicit. For both blame and prevention, we coded whether the assignment of responsibility was explicit or implicit. For both, in both years, the overwhelming tendency was for the designation of responsibility to be explicit (75 percent or more of the time).[9]

We speculated that television might, even if inadvertently, be more likely than print media to focus responsibility for hazards and hazard prevention on victims and other individuals rather than on institutions. As a visual medium, television might find it difficult to depict institutional responsibility. And indeed Iyengar, in his analysis, found that about 70 percent of television news stories were "episodic" rather than "thematic" (personal communication).

But there appeared to be no significant variations by media in the tendency to blame one or another source for a hazard. There was a suggestion that in stories about complex technology, television might be more likely to attribute responsibility for prevention to victims and other individuals: 12 percent of television stories

---

[9]The coding instructions undoubtedly played a role here. In the first place, if the story contained both explicit and implicit mentions, only the presence of explicit mentions was recorded. Second, coders were cautioned "that there should be something in the article that pointedly suggests a party's responsibility," because we did not want them to make unwarranted leaps of inference from the actual story content.

held victims or other individuals responsible for prevention, compared with no such stories in newspapers or newsweeklies. In the case of illness, this tendency was massively reversed: only 38 percent of television stories, compared with 63 percent of newsweekly and of newspaper stories, attributed responsibility for prevention to the victim or another individual.

Thus, we found no general tendency for television, any more than the other two media, to focus responsibility for prevention on victims rather than on social agencies. But because of our method of coding, we cannot really tell whether it is social institutions, or certain individuals in those institutions (e.g., safety directors or chief executive officers) who are held accountable by one or another medium. An interesting example of blaming individuals within institutions—and thereby trying to evade systemic responsibility—occurred during the 1992 Chicago flood. Within a couple of weeks of the crisis, Mayor Daley's investigation pinpointed only delinquent individuals (no structural flaws) for the disaster.

VOLUNTARY AND INVOLUNTARY EXPOSURE TO HAZARDS

Slovic, Fischhoff, and Lichtenstein (1979) have identified the voluntary or involuntary nature of exposure as an important determinant of public attitudes toward hazards of various kinds. And Hohenemser, Kates, and their colleagues (1983) similarly identify voluntary vs. involuntary exposure as one of a number of components that determine a hazard's seriousness. Consequently, we coded this aspect of the hazards reported in the media in order to determine whether it had any discernible consequences or correlates so far as blame or responsibility for prevention was concerned.

Like so many other coding decisions, this one proved more complex to execute than we had anticipated. For example, a number of stories about the MIC disaster in Bhopal, India, and about an LNG explosion in Mexico made a point of saying that shantytowns had grown up around the plants after they had been built, in spite of warnings and even regulations to the contrary. But the news accounts also made clear the constraints placed on workers' residential choices. Did they voluntarily settle in the neighborhood of the chemical plants, thereby assuming some of the responsibility for the subsequent disasters, or were their choices constrained enough so that they should be regarded as involuntary?[10] We coded these decisions as "largely or entirely outside of the individual's control," recognizing that our decision on this point is arguable.

Obesity and chronic alcoholism, as well as cigarette smoking, afford still other examples. Although exposure to these hazards is recognized as psychologically driven, we nevertheless coded it as largely within the individual's control, because we wanted to distinguish it from exposure that was clearly involuntary (e.g., a person trapped in a house fire caused by someone else's smoking, or involuntary exposure to a hazard as a result of working in a particular occupation, such as shipbuilding).[11]

The results of these coding decisions are displayed in Table 6.5, which indicates, by hazard category and year, the number of news stories in which exposure to the hazard was largely or entirely within the individual's control.

With two exceptions the distributions are very similar across the two years. Illness and natural disasters were coded as entailing mostly involuntary risks, whereas activities involving benefits and costs, predictably, were overwhelmingly coded as voluntary. Energy hazards, which often result from freely chosen activities, were likewise coded as entailing voluntary exposure about half the time.

Two categories of hazards—illness and complex technologies— show a sizable increase in the proportion of hazards coded as voluntary between 1960 and 1984. In both cases, however, this results from a different mix of specific hazards in the two years, and neither change is statistically significant.

[10] Ordinarily, we avoided having to make this kind of decision by asking what the media said. In the case of voluntary or involuntary exposure, however, we attempted to code whether exposure was voluntary or not regardless of what the media said or whether they said anything on this point at all.

[11] Whether "choosing" to work in such an industry after its hazards have been identified is voluntary or involuntary behavior is another difficult question, which we also resolved in favor of involuntary exposure. Though we had good reasons for all these decisions and tried to apply them consistently, it is plain that coding rules, which clearly affect the conclusions drawn, are all arbitrary to some extent, and in all likelihood reflect biases characteristic of the coders and/or contemporary U.S. society. For example, genetic factors in obesity and alcoholism are increasingly being recognized, and in the future exposure to these hazards may well be characterized as involuntary.

TABLE 6.5 / Percentage of Stories in Which Exposure Was Voluntary, by Hazard and Year

			Year	
	1960[a]		1984[a]	
Hazard Category	(%)	(N)	(%)	(N)
Natural hazards	11.1	(27)	11.8	(102)
Activities with B/C	100.0	(4)	95.3	(43)
Energy hazards	55.1	(49)	46.2	(91)
Materials hazards	29.2	(24)	21.9	(178)
Complex technologies	16.7	(12)	39.8	(98)
Illnesses	12.8	(39)	24.0	(96)
TOTAL	31.0	(155)	32.2	(608)

[a]Differences between categories of hazard are significant by chi-square test; differences between years, controlling for hazard, are not.

It seemed likely that stories about hazards to which exposure is perceived as voluntary would blame the victim, whereas stories about involuntary exposure to a hazard would blame industry, government, or some other agent. And, in fact, these expectations were borne out by the data. Both in 1960 and in 1984, blame and responsibility for prevention tended to be focused on victims when exposure was seen as voluntary, and on other agents when it was not (see Tables 6.6, 6.7). In fact, in virtually no case of involuntary exposure was blame attributed to the victim. There is

TABLE 6.6 / Target of Blame, by Voluntary Exposure and Year[a]

	Victim		Others	
Exposure	(%)	(N)	(%)	(N)
			1960	
Voluntary	29.4	(17)	70.6	(17)
Involuntary	3.7	(54)	96.3	(54)
			1984	
	%	(N)	%	(N)
Voluntary	39.3	(117)	60.7	(117)
Involuntary	1.6	(247)	98.4	(247)

[a]The change from 1960 to 1984 is not significant for either voluntary or involuntary hazards (χ^2 for voluntary hazards, .27; for involuntary hazards, .40). Differences between voluntary and involuntary hazards are significant in both years.

TABLE 6.7 / Who Is Responsible for Prevention, by Voluntary Exposure and Year[a]

	Victim		Others	
Exposure	(%)	(N)	(%)	(N)
		1960		
Voluntary	28.6	(28)	72.4	(28)
Involuntary	15.4	(65)	84.6	(65)
		1984		
	(%)	(N)	(%)	(N)
Voluntary	38.9	(167)	61.1	(167)
Involuntary	5.7	(279)	94.3	(279)

[a]The change from 1960 to 1984 is not significant for voluntary hazards ($\chi^2 = .70$, $df = 1$). The change from 1960 to 1984 is significant for involuntary hazards and indicates that people were less likely to be held accountable in 1984 than in 1960 for preventing hazards to which they were involuntarily exposed ($\chi^2 = 6.93$, $df = 1$, $p < .01$). The difference between voluntary and involuntary hazards is significant in 1984 but not in 1960.

some indication in these tables that in cases of voluntary exposure the tendency to blame the victim, or to hold the potential victim responsible for prevention, increased between 1960 and 1984, though the changes fail to reach statistical significance.

REGULATION, LITIGATION, AND COST

With respect to some of the hazards featured in news accounts, the issue was not simply one of moral blame or responsibility but of actual or potential legal culpability as well. In order to monitor changes in this aspect of hazard reporting, we coded, for each hazard story analyzed in detail, whether or not there was a reference to regulation or litigation. Furthermore, since assuming responsibility may well involve an expenditure of money—for research, cleanup, containment, and so forth—we also coded whether or not the news story made any reference to the financial costs of containing, removing, or preventing the hazard.

The proportion of stories making some reference to regulation is shown in Table 6.8. In both 1960 and 1984, differences between hazard categories are significant, and most categories show an (insignificant) increase between 1960 and 1984. Television was less likely to refer to regulation than either of the other two media.

TABLE 6.8 / **Percentage of Stories Mentioning Regulation, by Hazard and Year**

	Year			
	1960[a]		1984[a]	
Hazard Category	(%)	(N)	(%)	(N)
Natural hazards	3.6	(28)	5.9	(102)
Activities with B/C	25.0	(4)	44.2	(43)
Energy hazards	30.6	(49)	42.4	(92)
Materials hazards	37.5	(24)	38.5	(179)
Complex technologies	50.0	(12)	32.7	(98)
Illnesses	2.5	(40)	15.5	(110)
TOTAL	21.0	(157)	29.2	(624)

[a]Differences between hazards are significant by chi-square test; differences between years, controlling for hazard, are not.

References to litigation, by hazard category and year, are shown in Table 6.9. On average, such references increased considerably in the twenty-four-year period: from 3.2 percent to 17.9 percent, a finding in line with perceptions of increasing litigiousness in U.S. society. In both years, references to litigation were disproportionately high in complex technology stories (which are largely, it will be remembered, stories about medical and biotechnology hazards). And in 1984 references to litigation were disproportionately high in stories about materials hazards. As we have

TABLE 6.9 / **Percentage of Stories Mentioning Litigation, by Hazard and Year**

	Year			
	1960[a]		1984[b]	
Hazard Category	(%)	(N)	(%)	(N)
Natural hazards	0.0	(28)	2.9	(102)
Activities with B/C	0.0	(4)	4.7	(43)
Energy hazards	2.0	(49)	2.2	(92)
Materials hazards	4.2	(24)	41.3	(179)
Complex technologies	16.7	(12)	23.5	(98)
Illnesses	2.5	(40)	5.2	(110)
TOTAL	3.2	(157)	17.9	(624)

[a]Cell sizes are too small to permit reliable calculation of chi-square.
[b]Differences between hazards are significant by chi-square test; differences between years, controlling for hazards, are significant only for materials hazards.

already noted, stories about materials hazards in 1984 included a large number about Bhopal, and 58.5 percent of all such stories contained a reference to litigation, compared with only 26.5 percent for other stories in this category. Even this, however, represents a substantial increase over such references in comparable stories in 1960. Compared with newsweeklies and television, newspapers were especially likely to include references to litigation, but this was because they included a far larger proportion of stories about materials hazards (data not shown).

It is clear that for most hazards reported on in the press, responsibility is allocated informally rather than formally. Whereas a large majority of stories implicate someone or something as responsible for the hazard or its prevention, only a minority indicate that this responsibility is rooted in formal regulations or is legally enforceable (see Tables 6.1, 6.2, 6.8, and 6.9).

References to costs, finally, are shown in Table 6.10, again by hazard category and year. Paralleling the increase in references to regulation and litigation, there is an average increase in such references between 1960 and 1984. But the largest increase, in stories about natural hazards, is attributable to references to the cost of famine relief in stories about Ethiopia. Thus, once again, changes in hazard reporting appear to have more to do with changes in the particular hazards reported on than do changes in the reporting practices themselves.

TABLE 6.10 / **Percentage of Stories Mentioning Financial Cost, by Hazard and Year**

	Year			
	1960[a]		1984[b]	
Hazard Category	(%)	(N)	(%)	(N)
Natural hazards	0.0	(28)	34.3	(102)
Activities with B/C	0.0	(4)	2.3	(43)
Energy hazards	10.2	(49)	9.8	(92)
Materials hazards	16.7	(24)	10.1	(179)
Complex technologies	75.0	(12)	52.0	(98)
Illnesses	2.5	(40)	15.6	(110)
TOTAL	12.1	(157)	20.7	(624)

[a]Cell sizes are too small to permit reliable calculation of chi-square.
[b]Differences between hazards are significant by chi-square test; differences between years, controlling for hazards, are significant only for natural hazards and illnesses.

SUMMARY AND CONCLUSION

The following conclusions can be drawn from the patterns of blame that appeared in news accounts of hazards in 1960 and in 1984:

First, about half of all news stories attribute no blame or responsibility for a hazard at all, either because the issue of blame is not salient or because responsibility is taken for granted, or perhaps for some other reason. The likelihood of assigning blame varies from one hazard category to another.

Second, patterns of blame vary depending on the type of hazard involved. It makes no sense to talk about a generalized tendency to blame the victim, for example, because such a tendency is found with respect to some types of hazards (e.g., illness and, especially, activities involving benefits and costs) but not with respect to others. One interesting question has to do with how often individuals within institutions, rather than the institutions as such, are held accountable for a hazard or its prevention, but unfortunately our coding system did not allow us to make this distinction.

Third, responsibility for a hazard can be distinguished from responsibility for its prevention, and many more news accounts spell out responsibility for prevention than attribute blame for the hazard itself. Furthermore, as a little reflection makes obvious, the agents responsible for a hazard are not necessarily the same as those charged with its prevention. Again, as with blame, attribution of responsibility for prevention varies from one type of hazard to another.

Fourth, we found few changes in patterns of blaming between 1960 and 1984, and almost all those we did find were attributable to changes in the mix of specific hazards between the two years rather than to changes in reporting practices. For example, we found no greater tendency to blame victims for their illness in 1984 than in 1960, though such a tendency was more pronounced for AIDS than for other illnesses. Thus, there is no evidence from out study that cultural patterns of attributing blame for specific dangers have undergone any notable change in the last twenty-four years, at least insofar as these patterns are reflected in media reports.

Fifth, we had hypothesized that patterns of accountability for hazards where vested interests were involved (e.g., tobacco and alcohol) would tend to blame the victim and hold victims responsible for prevention. While this was, indeed, the pattern for these two hazards, it did not differ at all from the patterns of blame for other voluntary activities involving benefits and costs (e.g., skiing or contact sports). Thus, a more fruitful question may be how certain activities come to be defined as voluntary in the first place.

Sixth, the limited comparisons we were able to make between media indicated no differences between them in attributions of blame. Perhaps analysis of the TV images would have altered this conclusion, which is based only on the scripts, but the analysis by Wilkins and Patterson (1987:82–83) suggests that the specific medium may not be particularly relevant to the pattern of blame:

> Because news is based on the concept of novelty rather than situational analysis, car accidents, the product of a well-known risky system, seldom become major news stories, while leaks of methyl isocyanate in Bhopal or the partial meltdown of the Chernobyl power plant do. Because news is event-centered, it seldom looks at the system in which a given event is embedded. . . . Add to these structural elements the professional demands to "humanize" individual stories, and news reports of risk make what Fischhoff (1984) has called the fundamental attribution error: "the tendency to attribute too much responsibility to people for their actions and too little to the social and environmental constraints shaping those behaviors."

The analysis of blame in this chapter is limited in at least two ways. First, as we have already noted, while attributions of blame could be explicit or implicit, they had to be specifiable precisely enough so that coders could agree on the classification. Consequently, some implicit attributions may have been missed. Second, though we coded the targets of blame for each story, we did not, because of the diversity of hazards encountered, attempt a subtler breakdown. For example, we did not try to distinguish between stories that blamed the "irresponsibility of a few companies" and those that blamed the conflicts inherent in a capitalist system. In both cases, industry was coded as the target of blame.

7 / The Use of Sources in the Reporting of Hazards

Journalists are the public's eyes on the world, but journalists themselves are rarely eyewitnesses. Even when they are eyewitnesses, convention dictates that they tell the story primarily through sources rather than through their own observations. And so one point all analysts agree upon is the indispensable role of people as sources for the journalistic enterprise.

Journalists need to be keen observers, but they need even more to be keen identifiers, selectors, and cultivators of people as sources. A reporter who had prepared a standard news story, relying entirely on his own, even astute eyewitness description, would almost certainly be asked, "Where are the quotes?" But a reporter who pieces together a story entirely from source accounts, without leaving the newsroom, is not necessarily asked, "Why weren't you there?"

Two of the major discussions of newswork and source-journalist relationships are Bernard Roshco's *Newsmaking* and Herbert Gans's *Deciding What's News*. While Roshco directed his attention particularly to national political reporting, his analysis pertains broadly to newsmaking in general. The most highly valued sources are "individuals with authoritative personal knowledge regarding significant events" (1975:74). Sources become more newsworthy as they become more powerful and thus enlarge their scope of authoritative knowledge. Roshco traces journalists' inclination to personalize the news to their reliance on source-individuals: though sources are often newsworthy only because of their institutional position, the compelling point here is that sources are individuals, not institutions.

Given their need for sources as their "surrogate observers," reporters are ordinarily willing participants in a system where sources "manage" the information, not in a heavy-handed, censorious way but in a more routine, less obtrusive way. Sources continually decide whether information should be revealed, what details should be highlighted or discarded, when a story should be offered. "The sine qua non," writes Roshco, "[for the source's continued success] at controlling news content is not to remind the press it participates in a process [of news management] to which it usually assents" (p. 86). It is only when the source's routine low-key control of the news is replaced by blatant manipulation and suppression that reporters raise protests over the usually consensual collaboration.

In his discussion of sources and reporters, Gans draws on two metaphors to describe their relations. The first is that of a tango: it does "take two to tango," but sources tend to lead; and the second is that of a tug-of-war.

As Gans points out, journalists pursue only a small number of all potential or would-be sources. Who are the individuals who get tapped as actual sources? Gans identifies two factors that enter the calculus: (1) source availability or access, and (2) source suitability or newsworthiness. Once someone does become a source, he or she may manage the content, but of course journalists are forever striving to elicit more information from sources than they may want to give. In the final news report, it is the journalists who pick and choose which sources and which material from their sources to incorporate into their copy. But they can select only from those sources who have been willing to participate, and only from information the sources have disclosed. Of course, good reporters hone their ability to play sources off against one another—subtly in most cases, but more aggressively when necessary. But that very byplay simply underscores the journalist's reliance on sources. Gans characterizes news organizations as unique among commercial firms in that the raw material for the product they sell is obtained without charge. And this characteristic is etched normatively in the journalists' canon of ethics, which proscribes checkbook journalism.[1]

Gans and Roshco capture some of the basic conditions and considerations that motivate, propel, and shape source-journalist interaction. This condensed account of that interaction provides the background for our particular interest in sources. Our questions are not directed at source-journalist relations. Instead, we are interested in how the kinds of sources used are linked to reporting about hazards. We begin by identifying the different kinds of sources quoted in news stories about hazards. With those basic descriptive data in hand, we then explore the relationship between kinds of sources and other characteristics of the news story: the detail with which information about hazards is reported, the inclusion of conflicting assessments of hazard risks, and the presence of recommendations for hazard alleviation.[2]

WHAT KINDS OF SOURCES ARE QUOTED IN NEWS STORIES ABOUT HAZARDS?

We coded each story for the presence of nine different kinds of sources (plus an "other" category). The number of stories citing each kind of source is shown in Table 7.1. The number of stories

[1]Until very recently, the same was true of polling organizations, which relied on the cooperation of the public to provide the raw material of public opinion polls. But increasing resistance to being interviewed has led polling organizations increasingly to offer payment of some sort, especially if the interview is long or otherwise burdensome.

[2]While these hypotheses are quite general, others (e.g., Stallings, 1990) have postulated a much more specific link between sources and the depiction of risk. Stallings, for example, notes that news accounts of deteriorating bridges in the United States published in the *New York Times* "contain two distinctly different views of causation. One depicts the causes of collapses and other deficiencies as acts of nature. The other sees causation in terms of human agency" (p. 182). He asks why some, rather than other, causes enter into media discourse, and concludes that the answer lies in the selection of news sources, whose words are "transformed by reporters and editors into sentences, paragraphs, and headlines. . . . Put simply, the selection of an image of risk—including patterns of causation—takes place in the selection of news sources" (p. 190).

TABLE 7.1 / Sources Cited, by Year

	1960		1984	
Kind of Source	(%)	(N)	(%)	(N)
University scientist	18.4	(32)	7.3	81
Government scientist	8.0	(14)	6.0	67
Industry scientist	4.0	(7)	2.1	24
Lobbyist	6.3	(11)	7.1	79
Government official	27.0	(47)	20.9	233
Industry spokesperson	5.2	(9)	12.3	137
Hospital spokesperson	5.7	(10)	7.3	81
Victim	2.3	(4)	7.6	85
Potential victim	0.5	(1)	4.8	54
Other source	22.4	(39)	24.7	276
TOTAL	99.8	(174)	100.1	(1,117)

$$X^2 = 47.38; df = 9; p < .01$$

does not add up to the total number of stories analyzed, because more than one type of source could be coded for each story.

As can be seen from Table 7.1, government officials are far and away the type of source most frequently quoted in these stories: 27.0 percent of the sources quoted were government officials in 1960, and 20.9 percent in 1984. The next most frequently quoted source was university scientists in 1960, and industry spokespersons in 1984. "Other" sources represented an assortment of personal sources used by journalists in these stories. Although together they make up a sizable fraction of all the sources quoted, no single category was large enough to warrant its addition to the list of codes shown in Table 7.1. Although we have not done a comparative analysis, it is our impression that government officials are, in fact, the source most frequently quoted by journalists in general. In fact, news is often described by students of the press as "official" news, or news biased by journalists' excessive dependence on the official version of events put out by government spokespersons (Gans, 1979; Diamond, 1984).

Both university scientists and government officials were quoted relatively more often in 1960 than in 1984, whereas industry spokespersons and victims, whether actual or potential, were quoted more often in 1984 than in 1960. Although the citing of victims and potential victims suggests some movement away from the official version of events, the greater attention accorded industry spokespersons suggests instead a move from one institutional setting to another.

The frequency with which different sources were quoted in different types of media, by year, is shown in Table 7.2. In 1960 newsweeklies were somewhat less likely than newspapers to quote lobbyists and government officials (2.0 percent vs. 12.0 percent and 21.2 percent vs. 34.7 percent, respectively); industry spokespersons, on the other hand, were quoted more often (8.1 percent vs. 1.3 percent). In 1984 newspapers again showed a greater reliance on government sources than the other media (24.7 percent vs. 15.9 percent for weeklies and 18.6 percent for television), whereas television was more likely to quote victims or potential victims than either of the other media. The decreased reliance on government officials and increased use of industry spokespersons, already noted in Table 7.1, is here seen to be common to both newspapers and newsmagazines, as is the decline in reliance on university scientists, a trend we did not anticipate and have no explanation for. But because of the small cell sizes, the findings for 1960 should be regarded as suggestive only.

THE RELATIONSHIP OF SOURCES TO OTHER CHARACTERISTICS OF THE NEWS STORY

We formulated the following hypotheses about the variety of sources used by journalists and other characteristics of news stories about hazards:

1. Because of what we perceived as a general movement toward more specialized knowledge, we predicted that journalists would quote a greater variety of sources in 1984 than in 1960.

2. The greater the variety of sources used, the greater the wealth of detail we expected to be provided about hazards.

3. The greater the variety of sources used, we reasoned, the greater the likelihood of conflicting statements within the news story, and the greater the number of issues about which conflicting statements appear.

4. We expected the likelihood of conflicting points of view appearing within the same story to vary significantly from one type of source to another.

TABLE 7.2 / Sources Cited, by Media and Year

| | 1960[a] | | | | 1984[b] | | | | | | |
| Kind of Source | Newspapers | | Weeklies | | Newspapers | | Weeklies | | TV | |
	(%)	(N)	(%)	(N)	(%)	(N)	(%)	(N)	(%)	(N)
University scientist	18.7	(14)	18.2	(18)	7.7	(40)	11.0	(27)	4.0	(14)
Government scientist	6.7	(5)	9.1	(9)	5.8	(30)	8.5	(21)	4.5	(16)
Industry scientist	4.0	(3)	4.0	(4)	2.5	(13)	3.7	(9)	0.6	(2)
Lobbyist	12.0	(9)	2.0	(2)	7.5	(39)	8.1	(20)	5.6	(20)
Government official	34.7	(26)	21.2	(21)	24.7	(128)	15.9	(39)	18.6	(66)
Industry spokesperson	1.3	(1)	8.1	(8)	13.5	(70)	13.4	(33)	9.6	(34)
Hospital spokesperson	4.0	(3)	7.1	(7)	5.8	(30)	7.3	(18)	9.3	(33)
Victim	—	(—)	4.0	(4)	4.8	(25)	8.1	(20)	11.3	(40)
Potential victim	—	(—)	1.0	(1)	2.9	(15)	3.7	(9)	8.5	(30)
Other	18.7	(14)	25.3	(25)	24.7	(127)	20.3	(50)	28.0	(99)
TOTAL	100.1	(75)	100.0	(99)	99.9	(517)	100.0	(246)	100.0	(354)

[a] Cell sizes are too small to permit reliable calculation of chi-square.
[b] Differences between media are significant; $X^2 = 70.06$, $df = 18$, $p < .01$.

5. The greater the variety of sources used, the greater the number of recommendations concerning the hazard that we expected to appear in the news story.

Hypothesis 1: Journalists will quote a greater variety of sources in 1984 than in 1960.

Our first hypothesis is based on the explosion of group interests that has taken place since the sixties: the birth and growth of the civil rights movement, the women's movement, the gay and lesbian rights movement, the fight for the rights of the disabled. This development, we assumed, would be associated with the incorporation of more varied perspectives into stories about hazards, as indeed into other kinds of stories.

In order to test this hypothesis, we coded the number of different kinds of sources quoted by the journalist, not the absolute number of different sources. So, for example, five university scientists quoted in one story would be counted as only one kind of source, whereas one university scientist and one industry scientist in the same story would be counted as two kinds of sources. The reason for this way of looking at sources is that we were interested in how many different perspectives journalists brought to bear in their stories, and we assumed that sources occupying different social statuses would bring more varied perspectives to bear than those occupying a single status, even if there were several of the latter.

Our first hypothesis was supported by the data. Journalists indeed quoted a greater variety of sources in 1984 than they had in 1960. This was true for all categories of hazard combined, and for each category considered individually. The average number of different kinds of sources quoted was 1.79 in 1984, compared with 1.11 in 1960.

Both in 1960 and in 1984, the number of different kinds of sources quoted varied significantly from one hazard category to another.[3] In both years, stories about materials hazards quoted a greater variety of sources than stories about other hazards. In 1960, this was also true for stories about energy hazards, and in 1984 it was true as well for stories about complex technologies.

[3] In 1960, $F (5, 151) = 2.365$; $p < .05$; in 1984, $F (5, 618) = 6.832$, $p < .01$.

Hypothesis 2: The greater the number of different kinds of sources used, the greater the wealth of detail provided about the hazard.

In Chapter 5 we reported on the kinds of information presented about hazards, asking in particular whether accounts in the press provided any information about six of the twelve dimensions of hazard singled out as important by Hohenemser and his colleagues (1983): annual mortality, size of population at risk, spatial extent, delay in onset of consequences, persistence of the hazard, and transgenerational effects. We found that, in general, very little information was provided about such characteristics in the press (see Chapter 5, pages 84–90).

However, our second hypothesis was supported by the data. Those stories that used a greater variety of sources also provided more information (as measured by the number of details given) about hazard characteristics than stories citing fewer kinds of sources ($F(1, 467) = 12.799; p < .01$). As an example of the former, a *Newsweek* story (Dec. 24, 1984) about a South Dakota town volunteering to store low-level radioactive waste quoted geologists, government officials, industry spokespersons, and members of the public. It made reference to the size of the population at risk, the spatial extent of the hazard, its actual or expected persistence, as well as the possibility of transgenerational effects.

Hypothesis 3: The greater the variety of sources used, the greater the likelihood of conflicting statements within the news story, and the greater the number of issues about which conflicting statements appear.

We were especially interested in the extent to which news stories about hazards portrayed conflicting views concerning such things as the likelihood that the hazard would occur; that if it occurred, it would cause harm; that adequate precautions could be taken against it; and who was responsible for the hazard (or for taking precautions against it).[4] An analysis of variance with number of sources, type of hazard, and year as predictor vari-

---

[4]Coders were asked to indicate whether or not the story mentioned conflicting opinions about any of these issues.

ables, and the presence of conflicting statements as the dependent variable indicates significant effects for all three predictors, thus providing support for hypothesis 3: the greater the variety of sources, the greater the likelihood of conflicting statements in the news story. Stories about materials hazards and complex technologies were more likely to contain some conflicting statements than stories about other categories of hazard (51.4 percent and 55.1 percent, respectively, compared with an average of about 35 percent for stories about other types of hazard). And conflicting views were less likely to appear in 1960 than in 1984 (they appeared in 18.4 percent of stories in 1960, compared with 40.5 percent of those in 1984).

We had also hypothesized that stories drawing on a greater variety of sources would contain conflicting views about a greater number of issues, and this hypothesis, too, was supported. The effect of sources is highly significant, even controlling for the effects of hazard category and year ($F(1, 768) = 118.947$, $p < .01$). An example is a front-page story about Dutch treatment of heroin addicts ("Controversy Surrounds the Way the Dutch Treat Heroin Addicts," *Wall Street Journal*, Dec. 5, 1984), in which the reporter sought out scientists, government officials, drug addicts, and a caseworker and presented divergent opinions about a number of risk-related issues—the likelihood that the treatment method would encourage the spread of heroin addiction, the harmfulness of the addiction, and the costs of alternative treatment methods.

This association between number of sources and likelihood of conflicting opinions appearing in the news story does not, of course, mean that conflicting views necessarily result from citing a larger variety of sources. It may be that journalists, knowing a hazard entails disputed issues, seek out sources to comment on different sides of the dispute. Nor does the citing of a large number of sources necessarily mean greater enlightenment for the reader or viewer. On the contrary, it may simply reinforce the sense of uncertainty and confusion unless readers or viewers are given some guidance about the credibility of the various sources cited by the journalist.

Stories about two hazard types, activities involving benefits and costs and complex technologies, carried conflicting statements about a greater number of issues than stories about other hazards.

And 1984 stories contained conflicting statements about a wider variety of issues than those in 1960, even controlling for the number of different kinds of sources used (MCA analysis, data not shown).

Hypothesis 4: The likelihood of conflicting points of view will vary according to the type of source quoted in the news story.

Stories in which government officials are quoted as sources were no more likely than others to contain conflicting versions of events. In fact, conflicting views were expressed somewhat less often in these stories than in stories citing many other kinds of sources, a situation which accords with the impression that the use of official sources may entail a certain establishment bias. Note that the category of government official excludes scientists employed by the government, who are also quoted in a substantial number of stories. Citing of spokespersons for lobbying organizations, on the other hand, was associated with somewhat higher levels of conflict, suggesting that journalists are more careful to balance the views of such groups with others that may be at odds with them. For example, a *Time* story (Dec. 17, 1984) about toxic chemicals in the U.S. in the wake of the MIC release in Bhopal, India, quoted not only public interest groups but also spokespersons for industry and government officials in examining the issues raised by storage and transportation of such chemicals across the country. A front-page *Wall Street Journal* story on the same issues (Dec. 14, 1984) followed a similar pattern.

Not unexpectedly, stories citing victims or potential victims as sources contained the highest level of conflict of all. Although victims or potential victims were quoted relatively infrequently, stories that did so were likely to include conflicting views 54.4 percent and 56.4 percent of the time. The average level of conflict in stories citing other sources was around 41 percent.[5]

When conflicting points of view are presented in a news story, do the media give readers or viewers any clue about which opin-

---

[5]This is one of the few findings where weighting the data makes a difference. In the weighted data set, stories in which victims and potential victims are cited manifest conflict 51.6 percent and 57.9 percent of the time, compared with an average of around 49 percent for other sources—a much smaller difference.

ion is to be given more weight? About half the time they do (newspapers: 63 percent, N = 135; newsweeklies: 52.6 percent, N = 76; television: 49.3 percent, N = 71), by direct evaluation, by the adjectives used (e.g., referring to someone as a "maverick scientist"), by the space and prominence given to a quote, or by some other means or combination of means. For example, CBS opened a story (Oct. 3, 1984) on the risks associated with working in nuclear weapons plants by quoting from a worker "who was dying when he recorded these words." Although the story later quotes government scientists in refutation, we suspect that the viewer is more likely to recall the impact of the dying worker's assessment than the scientists' denial. The *Wall Street Journal* story cited above in connection with the risk posed by toxic chemicals conveys its sense of threat by the space and prominence given to a discussion of the risks these chemicals pose to life and property, as well as by direct recommendations concerning future policy.

Hypothesis 5: The greater the variety of sources used, the greater the number of different action recommendations concerning the hazard that are included in the story.

We coded each news story with respect to the recommendations for action it contained. Specifically, we coded recommendations concerning the prevention of the hazard, relief for hazard victims, and further research. The only factor significantly related to the number of action recommendations was the type of hazard,[6] with stories about natural disasters containing more action recommendations than stories about other types of hazards, and stories about complex technologies containing fewer. Neither the number of sources nor the year had a statistically significant effect.[7]

THE USE OF PUBLISHED SOURCES

So far, we have discussed the type of source most frequently used by journalists: a quotable person. Very few of the news sto-

[6]F (5, 273) = 8.651, $p < .01$.
[7]For this analysis we used a version of the variable that standardizes the proportion of action recommendations across hazard categories.

TABLE 7.3 / Number of News Stories[a] Citing Research, by Year

| | 1960 | | 1984 | |
	(%)	(N)	(%)	(N)
Research cited	30.6	(157)	27.9	(624)
Published source cited	16.7	(48)	24.7	(174)
Researcher named	60.4	(48)	54.0	(174)

[a]The number of stories includes issue stories only.

ries we monitored made reference to a published source, the kind of source much more familiar to social scientists.

The number of news stories that made some reference to research related to a hazard or its prevention in 1960 and 1984 is shown in Table 7.3. The percentage of all stories is just about the same in both years: 30.6 percent in 1960, and 27.9 percent in 1984. For these stories, we coded whether the journalist made reference to a published source, and whether he or she referred to a named social scientist. Those figures, too, are shown in Table 7.3. Relatively small proportions of journalists in both years, and somewhat fewer in 1960 than in 1984, made reference to a published source. More than twice as many journalists in 1984, and almost four times as many journalists in 1960, made reference to a named social scientist in connection with the cited research.

For most of the stories citing published research, and for a few of those citing named researchers, we were able to locate the original research reports and compare them with the news story for accuracy. The results of this study of accuracy in hazard reporting are presented in the following chapter.

8 / How Accurately Do the Media Report on Risk?[1]

We have argued earlier that for certain classes of hazards, especially those that are both serious and rare, the media are the most likely source of information for most people. Furthermore, the media in question are not science or technical journals but the mass media, which draw on these other more specialized sources (e.g., the *New England Journal of Medicine* or *Environmental Hazards*) for newsworthy material for their audiences.

As a result, what the mass media report about hazards—which ones they select for emphasis and what information they present about them—becomes crucial in shaping public perceptions of hazards and their attendant risks. We need only recall Legionnaire's disease, toxic shock syndrome, or EDB to realize that this is true. In earlier chapters, we have considered some of these questions of selection and emphasis. In the present chapter we consider the accuracy of what is reported. Because that is an al-

[1]An earlier version of this chapter appeared as "A Question of Accuracy: How Journalists and Scientists Report Research on Hazards," in *Journal of Communication* 40(4) (1990):102–116. We would like to thank S. Holly Stocking for her thoughtful critique of the manuscript.

most unmanageably large task, we decided to narrow it by looking at one particular type of accuracy: reporting on research relating to hazards. The plan was to select a small subsample of all the news stories originally coded—perhaps fifty to sixty of them, spread over all six hazard categories—that contained a reference to research, and to compare the news story with the original research report.

The study of reporting accuracy has a venerable history of more than fifty years, ably reviewed by Meyer (1988). Meyer himself has recently added an innovative study to this history, one stressing the reliability of the resulting measures.[2] Because of his interest in reliability, Meyer uses a relatively narrow definition of accuracy. He does not, for example, inquire into the accuracy of the story as a whole, but only that part of it which is based on an interview with a particular source. Further, again in the interests of reliability, Meyer eschews asking about the more subjective aspects of accuracy, which are notorious for eliciting unreliable judgments.

Shapiro's account of the world of the fact checker at two general newsmagazines and one sports publication (1989) is another recent contribution to the study of reporting accuracy. Shapiro makes clear that what is actually checked—and also, equally important, what sources are accepted for verification purposes—severely limits the meaning of the accuracy guaranteed by fact checking. For example, although 80 percent of the objective statements checked agreed with the information in the source used, these sources included earlier news accounts, which may not have been correct either. Nor are the reporter's interview notes verified independently. And whether or not individual statements, even if accurate, yield an accurate news account, much less a true one,

---

[2]Meyer queried one randomly selected source for every bylined story on the local page of the newspaper with respect to four issues: accuracy of basic facts, accuracy of other facts, fairness (balance), and accuracy of quotes. Meyer then submitted each complaint to the offending reporter. Where reporter and source disagreed, the disputes were resolved by two coders. The net error rate resulting from this method was 11 percent, and generalizes to the newspaper's sources, not stories. Meyer points out that this method is designed to maximize validity and reliability for newspapers that wish to make accuracy evaluation an ongoing management tool and adds, "None of these proposals is intended to reflect on the good work of the many academicians who press more deeply into the accuracy problem."

is a question outside the fact checkers' sphere of responsibility, even though, as Shapiro is careful to point out, they often do their best to assure fairness, balance, and evidentiary standards as well.

Studies of accuracy in science reporting, an area closer to our own concerns than general news stories, have generally asked scientists to evaluate the news stories based on their work (e.g., Tankard and Ryan, 1974; McCall and Stocking, 1982; McCall, 1988; Weiss and Singer with Endreny, 1988). The errors cited in such studies are most often omissions and changes in emphasis rather than incorrect statements. For example, the scientists asked by Tankard and Ryan (1974) to evaluate reports of their work most frequently cited as errors the omission of relevant information about method and results, the misquoting of investigators, the omission of the names of other investigators on the research team, misleading headlines, an investigator being quoted out of context, ignoring the research's continuity with earlier work, and the story's being too brief.

All of these earlier studies have focused on accuracy as perceived by the scientist source. But, as McCall (1988) points out, research on accuracy that is based on the perceptions of the source is limited by the subjective nature of the task. Our study attempts to bypass this limitation by focusing directly on a comparison between the original research report, on the one hand, and its treatment in the popular press, on the other. Our goal was to take an ideal case—the existence of a published research report as a source—to investigate the types of errors and the extent of accurate "translation" of such research in news reports aimed at the general public.

METHODS

To study accuracy, we began by identifying those news stories in the sample that had been coded as containing a reference to research.[3] Because we wanted to carry out an objective comparison, rather than relying on the scientist's evaluation of whether

---

[3]The coding manual stipulated that only a "systematic, scientific examination of a problem, not just an ad hoc investigation or casual collection of data" should be coded as a reference to "research."

his or her work had been accurately reported, we limited the investigation to those news stories referring to a published source (any documentary source other than a press release) or to a written report that we could obtain independently.[4]

Our analysis of reporting accuracy is based on 42 news stories about hazards and their underlying reports by scientists.[5] Of these, 15 (36 percent) are illness stories, 4 (10 percent) are about complex technology, 7 (17 percent) are about materials hazards, 3 (7 percent) are about energy hazards, 7 (17 percent) are about activities with benefits and costs, and 6 (14 percent) are about natural hazards.[6] They are twice as likely to be drawn from newspapers as from either television or newsmagazines, but newsmagazines carry a higher proportion of research-based hazard stories than either of the other media. Interestingly enough, even though we identified 10 television news stories based on research, these represented only 4 different research reports. There was much less overlap among newspapers and newsmagazines.

The accuracy of these news stories was evaluated along eleven dimensions that were grouped under three main headings: outright error (inaccurate reference to a published source or substantially different statement), nonsubstantive alterations (changes of

---

[4]One type of story not analyzed here, even though it contains references to research, is a subset of science stories referring so vaguely to research or studies that it is impossible to track them down without help from the reporter. After a lapse of four years, we had to let such news stories go. However, we would argue that that is bad reporting practice, and that sources should always be identified clearly enough to permit checking.

[5]Of the fifty-one stories coded as referring to published research, we randomly deleted six illness stories because we wanted no more than fifteen of these. Two other stories concerning illness that were published in the sixties were replaced with stories from the eighties. Six stories were deleted because each devoted only one or two lines of a much longer story to the published research; two were deleted because they were based on studies identified vaguely or not at all; one was deleted because it was based only on an interview, not on published research; and one was deleted because we could not locate the study referred to. We augmented this sample of thirty-three stories with twenty-six stories coded as referring to a named researcher. We had to delete seventeen of these, mostly because they referred only to unidentified studies or made only passing reference to a study. As a result, we ended with a sample of forty-two news stories and their underlying research reports, all but three of them from 1984.

[6]As can be seen, stories based on published research come disproportionately from illness stories. Illness stories in general made up 11 percent of the population of hazard stories, but 36 percent of the stories involving research. On the other hand, energy stories made up 39 percent of the population of hazard stories, but only 7 percent of the research stories. Percentages for the other hazards were similar in the population and in the sample of stories based on research.

emphasis, misleading headline, translation, less precise formulation, and presentation of speculation as fact), and omissions (of important results, qualifying details, details of methods, and resulting overgeneralization). Judging from earlier research, these seemed to be the major dimensions of accurate reporting. A copy of the Accuracy Coding Form is included in Appendix C.

The senior author and a research assistant[7] independently coded all but five of the news stories and then reconciled any disagreements that existed between them. The overall level of agreement was 94 percent, and ranged from a low of 78 percent[8] to a high of 100 percent on individual questions. On some crucial items, such as whether or not any statements were substantially different from those in the research report, whether the emphasis was faithful to the original, and whether the headline was inaccurate, agreement ranged from 92 percent to 100 percent. (Although the research assistant was an undergraduate student with some experience as a journalist, the analysis is probably biased in favor of social scientific rather than journalistic conceptions of accuracy.)

Like all earlier studies of accuracy in science reporting, this one does not address the scientific validity of the underlying research. As reporter Lawrence K. Altman (1988) has pointed out, such an omission is a real weakness, and one that should be remedied in future research. Here, however, we confine ourselves to asking how accurately the original research was reported in the press. Nor do we care what materials were actually used by the reporter in writing the story. So long as a published report is mentioned in the account, we believe the appropriate comparison for assessing accuracy is the report itself.

FINDINGS

Outright Error

To begin with, it is worth noting that these news stories about hazards made a substantial number of errors of commission. Two

---

[7] We would like to thank Cydnee Blattner for her very competent execution of this task.

[8] Only one item had a reliability as low as this: "How many statements of fact in the news story are based on the original source?" Only tangential use was made of this item in the analysis.

practices were coded as outright errors. The first type is an incorrect reference to the published study—that is, a seemingly unambiguous reference that we were unable to trace at all (not just an error in date of publication, for example). Such an error may be relatively innocent—the other facts in the news story may be correct, and the study may have appeared in a journal other than the cited one—or it may be indicative of more serious, substantive errors. At the least, the reader who wants to track down the original source is prevented from doing so.

One of the stories we originally selected turned out to be erroneous in this sense and therefore had to be dropped from the sample, leaving forty-two stories for further analysis. That story, an article in *New York* magazine (Oct. 15, 1984, p. 74) headlined "Bypassing the Bypass," refers to a study in a "recent issue" of the *American Journal of Cardiology* indicating that blood flow is improved in three out of four patients undergoing angioplastic surgery. We were unable to find any such study in the 1982, 1983, or 1984 issues of the journal; because of the lapse of time, we were unable to go back to the reporter's files.

The second type of error of commission occurs when one or more of the statements in the news story is substantially different from a statement in the original research report. (Although the judgment of what is "substantially different" is subjective, the two coders agreed on it 92 percent of the time.) Such errors are not infrequent, occurring in 40 percent of stories (seventeen out of forty-two). (We did not bother to code such potential errors as misspellings, grammatical errors, omission of some authors' names, and the like.)

For example, an NBC news story (#0156)[9] said that researchers "studied 133 men who suffered massive heart attacks while exercising." In fact, they studied men who suffered cardiac arrest; only 9 of the 133 had actually suffered a heart attack while exercising. In another example from the same news story, men who exercise regularly were said to have "suffered 40% fewer heart attacks."

---

[9]Numbers in parentheses refer to the ID numbers of the cases used for analysis. A complete list of these cases, together with a list of the scientific reports on which they are based, appears in Appendix C.

In fact, according to the research report, their relative risk was 40 percent, which means something else. A *Newsweek* story on the treatment of patients with Alzheimer's disease (#2224) said that three out of four improved; according to the original research report, all four improved. *Newsweek* described the patients as moderately impaired, while the journal article described this impairment as moderately severe to severe. An NBC news story referred to "AIDS victims," but the journal article included patients with AIDS-related complex (ARC) and healthy homosexuals as well as AIDS patient (#0180).

Fourteen of these 17 stories contained only one or two erroneous statements, but since the vast majority of news stories contained fewer than 15 statements based on the original source, and 16 (38 percent) of the news stories contained fewer than 7 such statements, the proportion of erroneous statements is not negligible. There is, not unexpectedly, a significant relationship between the number of statements based on the source and the number substantially different from the original. Of the 16 stories with fewer than 7 statements based on the source, 11, or 69 percent, had no substantially different statements; of the 26 stories with 7 or more statements based on the source, only 14 (52 percent) had no such statements.[10]

Because we believed that anonymous sources would be less likely to be held accountable for errors, we hypothesized that news stories by an identifiable reporter would be less likely to contain erroneous statements than stories based on a wire service report, totally unidentified stories, or unsigned columns. Our hypothesis was supported only in part. The 24 bylined news stories were indeed more accurate than the twelve unsigned ones (58

---

[10]However, one *Newsweek* story (Oct. 29, 1984, p. 122) which we deleted from the sample because only one sentence of a long piece referred to an identifiable study, seriously distorted that one sentence. The reporter included the following quote from a National Research Council study: "VDT's . . . are highly unlikely to be hazardous." The actual quotation is, "the levels of radiation emitted by VDT's . . . are highly unlikely to be hazardous." Since what is suspected of being hazardous about VDTs is not only radiation but the magnetic fields such devices generate, this truncated quote is clearly misleading.

percent vs. 43 percent), but the six wire-service stories were the most accurate of all (100 percent).[11]

We also hypothesized that, because they suffer from fewer space/time constraints, print media would be more accurate than television. But again we were only partially correct. Newspaper stories were the most accurate, with 76 percent of 21 newspaper stories containing no statements substantially different from the source. This was true of 50 percent of the 10 TV stories but of only 36 percent of the 11 newsweekly stories. There were no consistent differences in accuracy by hazard category.

Nonsubstantive Alterations

So far, we have been talking about outright error. But many of the discrepancies observed by us as well as by Tankard and Ryan involve omissions or nonsubstantive changes rather than outright error. The first discrepancy of this type is an emphasis in the news story that differs from that in the original research report. A change of emphasis occurred in nineteen of the forty-two stories, or 45 percent.

Often, the reason for the change in emphasis in the news story is readily understandable. For example, a *New York Times* story (#2981) based on an article on "fragile sites" in chromosomes devotes much more space to issues of utility, prevention, and implications for cancer diagnosis than the original report does. A similarly understandable change in emphasis occurs when the news story is much more dramatic and optimistic than the original—as, for example, in the *Newsweek* story (#2224) that reports on an experimental treatment for Alzheimer's disease, or a *Wall Street Journal* story (#2519) that reports improvement in six patients given an experimental drug for pneumonia associated with AIDS. The change in emphasis in these stories begins to verge on error, because it implies that a new treatment is at hand, whereas it is, in fact, in the earliest stages of clinical trials. But this may be less an issue of accuracy than an issue of truth or ethics.

---

[11] News stories based on peer-reviewed journals were more likely to have no inaccurate statements than stories based on other sources (65 percent vs. 45 percent), but we did not address the more interesting question of the accuracy of the articles in the peer-reviewed journals.

Another change in emphasis that comes close to error occurs in an NBC story (#0190) discussing the risk of drinking during pregnancy. The journal article talks only about growth retardation; the news story explicitly links below-average birthweight with possible mental retardation, which the journal article does not do.

Interestingly enough, five of the changes in emphasis portrayed the hazard as riskier than the original article, and five did the reverse. (The remaining nine changes had no risk implications.)

The second type of discrepancy, a misleading or inaccurate headline, is closely related to a change in emphasis, but lies still closer to outright error. We did not attempt to distinguish between misleading and inaccurate headlines. For television stories, the "headline" was the first sentence on the transcript.

Thirteen of forty-two stories (31 percent) were coded as containing a misleading or inaccurate headline. For example, one journal article reported on the isolation of the AIDS virus in the semen and saliva of a healthy homosexual man, and another reported on the isolation of the virus in the saliva of men with ARC and in homosexual men exposed to AIDS. The headline of the *Daily News* article about these reports (#2190) reads, "Healthy Carriers May Be Spreading AIDS." The headline of an article in the *Wall Street Journal* (#3294) reads, "Drug Blocks Virus Linked to AIDS, Researchers Report," but the tests were *in vitro* only, and blocking was for nine days only. A CBS news story (#0188) began, "A study concludes that a pregnant woman taking even one or two drinks a day can endanger the health of her child," while the research report indicated that the birthweight of infants born to such women is lower than that of nondrinkers.

Often, but not always, stories with a misleading headline also were coded as changing the emphasis of the original research report. But most stories in which the emphasis departed from that of the original report (twelve of nineteen, or 63 percent) did not have a misleading or inaccurate headline.

Three other characteristics of hazards reporting fall under the general category of nonsubstantive changes. The first of these characteristics is *translation*, in which the statement, while not substantially different from the original, is written in an equivalent form better adapted to the reader's or viewer's linguistic habits.

Translation, as one might imagine, occurred fairly frequently, in 33 percent of the stories. For example, "Under general anesthesia, patients were positioned and draped as for ventriculoperitoneal shunt placement. A small frontal craniotomy was done. . . . The intracranial catheter position was varied from patient to patient" becomes, in *Newsweek*'s translation (#2224), "First, they inserted a plastic catheter about the width of a pencil lead through a tiny hole drilled on top of the skull and into one of the ventricles, the fluid-filled chambers inside the brain." "The more accurate practice of fetal Ph scalp monitoring is still practiced" becomes, in a *Newsweek* story (#3301), "Far more accurate is analysis of the acidity of the baby's blood." "Grams" in a journal article becomes "ounces" in an NBC news story (#0190).

A second frequent practice is the translation of statements from the research report into statements that, while again not substantially different, are less precise. Fifteen of forty-two stories, or 36 percent, were coded as having one or more statements that were less precise than those in the original.

For example, an NBC news story (#9807) said, "By a margin of 2 to 1"; the article gave exact percentages, which were not precisely 2:1. A *New York Times* news story (#9741) stated that exercise stimulated certain blood factors; the original article named them precisely. An ABC news story (#0185) referred to 31,000 births; the research article stated that 31,604 were studied. (Here, 32,000 would have been a more accurate approximation, though we did not code the statement as substantially different on that account.) Another ABC news story (#0151) stated that risk is "higher" for men who exercise less; in the article, the risk was given as 56:1 for sedentary men and 5:1 for men who exercise more than 2½ hours a week.

Some cases of translation, of course, also involve a loss in precision; and at times the combination of translation into everyday language and less precise formulation of the original findings or methods may result in inaccuracy: the transformation of a statement into one that is substantially different from its original form. As already noted, the category "substantially different" is hard to define precisely; others may draw the line much more stringently than we have done. For example, is "The caffeine had little effect in cells that had adequate supplies of folic acid" substantially different from, "When cells were cultured in MEM (in the presence of folic acid and thymidine), with or without caffeine, fewer than 1 percent of the chromosomes had visible breaks"? (Coded as not substantially different.)

The third characteristic we distinguish here involves treating as fact what is presented in the original article as speculation. Presenting speculation as fact occurred much less often than translation—18 percent of the time.

For example, an ABC story (#0151) spoke of "a population of 1.25 million that *surely includes* hundreds of thousands of regular exercisers." In a CBS story (#0153), a cardiologist commented on a study of exercise and heart attacks: "Two or three times a week perhaps is enough to protect you," not only drawing the causal inference that exercise protects but suggesting the number of exercise sessions a week that may confer protection. Neither of these statements appeared in the original research report. In a *Newsweek* story (#2224), the "cholinergic hypothesis" becomes, "The treatment is based on the fact that (patients' brains are deficient in acetylcholine)." In a story in *Amsterdam News* (#9654), estimates of future poverty in New York City are treated as if they were inevitable, instead of projections of current demographic and socioeconomic trends.

Omission

News stories based on lengthy research reports are inevitably selective, often in one or more of three ways: they omit some results that are deemed less important, they omit some or all qualifications, and they overgeneralize the findings. Sixteen of the forty-two stories (38 percent) omitted some results that the coders considered important; 25 (60 percent) omitted some qualifying statements; and 36 percent overstated the generalizability of the results. There were no differences by media with respect to any of these tendencies, but 71 percent of bylined stories omitted qualifying statements, compared with only 44 percent of all others. And news stories with a byline were, if anything, more likely than others to omit important research results—42 percent of the former and 33 percent of the latter did so. This pattern suggests a difference in journalistic and social science norms: What's good journalistic practice may be bad social science practice, and vice versa.

Examples of omitting important results include an ABC story (#0185) omitting results of the effects of smoking on fetal size and reporting only the effects of drinking; a *New York Times* story (#2983) omitting the main findings of a research report (that chromosome breaks are enhanced in the presence of caffeine and retarded in the presence of folic acid), instead emphasizing the relevance of the work for diagnosing cancer predispositions; an NBC story (#0301) omitting the fact that silent heart attacks occur more often in women than in men; and a *Newsweek* story (#3301) omitting the fact that the distribution of Caesarian sections does not parallel the distribution of high-risk populations (C-sections are more often done in high-income areas).

Examples of omitting qualifying statements include an ABC story (#0185) that omitted all authors' statements of how the methods limit the generalizability of the findings (e.g., that the study is based on women's retrospective reports and on reported drinking in the first trimester only); a *Newsweek* (#2224) story that made no mention of side effects nor of the absence of a control group in research involving four Alzheimer's patients; a *Wall Street Journal* story (#2519) that omitted all authors' statements about the limitations of the study, which involved only six AIDS patients and no control group; and a *Newsweek* story (#3034) that omitted the statement that findings concerning boxing injuries and deaths may not apply in the current era, when conditions have changed.

One example of overstating the generalizability of results comes from a *Wall Street Journal* story (#2519) on the treatment of six patients with an experimental drug, DFMO, for a type of virulent pneumonia associated with AIDS. The story made no mention of the possible confounding effects of other drugs or the absence of a control group, and its implications are more optimistic than the research warrants. The same was true of the *Newsweek* story (#2224) about an experimental treatment for Alzheimer's disease. An ABC story (#0185) ignored the fact that findings were based on first-trimester drinking only and that drinking during the second trimester may have no, or fewer, effects.

The last type of omission to be discussed has to do with research methods. News accounts of scientific reports, being shorter and more colloquial than the originals, most consistently omitted discussion of the research methods used. Almost half of all news stories coded—twenty out of forty-two, or 48 percent—made no mention of research methods at all. Fifteen included partial but, in our judgment, inadequate information about methods; four gave partial but adequate accounts; and in three, some of the information about methods was actually in error. Although our definition of "adequate" is probably arbitrary, it is clear that the majority of news stories either make no mention of methods at all or include some details that are erroneous.

For example, the NBC news story about drinking and birthweight (#0190) gave no information about how confounding variables were controlled, made no mention of the fact that the women were questioned retrospectively, and said nothing about the fact that the study was based on the first trimester only. We considered this partial but inadequate information. A *New York Times* story (#2043) made no reference to the fact that patients underwent angiograms to evaluate blood flow. We considered this partial but adequate information. A *New York Times* story about cancer risk in siblings (#1455) left out information on how the sample was selected and how the actual cases were compared with the expected number. This was coded as partial but inadequate information. An ABC news story (#0151) refers to a "comparison group," but in fact the comparison group merely served to establish baselines for the amount of exercise engaged in by men of various ages; there was no comparison of the dead men with the control group. We coded this as erroneous information. An NBC story (#0156) stated that scientists studied 133 men who died while exercising; in fact, only 9 of these died while exercising.

Miscellaneous Findings

Some of the inaccuracies we found seem to result from the media's need to dramatize research findings. It is true that certain of the practices already described serve to heighten the dramatic impact of a science report—for example, omitting qualifications in a study, or overgeneralizing the results. Sometimes, however, even more explicit dramatic devices are used, as in this excerpt from a *Time* story (Dec. 24, 1984, p. 56):

It is two weeks after a major nuclear war, and the searing white flashes of 25,000 bombs have faded into a black drizzle of radioactive fallout. Yet Armageddon is not complete: for miles above the earth, sunlight is blotted out by plumes of smoke from the vast conflagrations in which the major cities of the Northern Hemisphere have been consumed.[12]

And so on, to the end of the paragraph. This is, of course, a free and highly dramatic translation from the text of the research report, which is a National Academy of Sciences study of the possibility of "nuclear winter" after a nuclear exchange. Is it inaccurate? What standards of accuracy, if any, should be applied to such a passage? As Wilkins and Patterson (1987:82) put it, "because the journalistic rendering of risk uses images that carry with them such strong cultural and emotional overtones, the translation of the mathematical precision of risk analysis is problematic."

Another common dramatic device, especially on television, is to begin a scientific report by exemplifying it in particular people—for example, beginning the fetal alcohol study by vignettes of two mothers, one who drinks and the other who doesn't, or the heart-attack-while-exercising study with an interview with the widow of a man who died while swimming. In the latter case, particularly, one can raise a question about what the viewer is likely to remember: the careful account of the study itself, which concludes that the benefits of exercise outweigh its costs, or the grieving widow's dramatic account of her husband's death while exercising?

One issue that has been raised about science reporting is that, in their quest for balance, journalists may overrepresent extremes. One of the panelists convened by Dunwoody and Friedman (1986) put it this way: "In our efforts to get all sides of a story, presenting fringe positions is inevitable." Another said, "I think that many times extremists are given too much space in stories because balance is missing. Sometimes the balance can only be supplied by reporters knowledgeable enough to know where to look for the other side of the story. Remember, too, that extremists can turn out to be right" (pp. 107–8).

Sixteen (28 percent) of the news stories we analyzed included

---

[12]We did not attempt to count the instances of dramatization illustrated here.

some comments by others. Ten of these carried supporting comments from other sources, and five carried comments that qualified the findings in some way. Only six carried comments that we classified as conflicting or challenging, and these were about an even smaller number of original research reports, whose findings were considered especially controversial. The proportions of comments in these stories are somewhat higher than those we found in a study of social science reporting (Weiss and Singer with Endreny, 1988). Whether the comments give undue prominence to conflicting "experts" is a question we unfortunately cannot answer here.

An example of a supporting comment occurred in a *Time* story (#1617) that quoted epidemiologist Reuel Stallones of the University of Texas, who contributed to a 1980 report from the National Academy of Sciences that found the human health hazards of antibiotic feeds "neither proven nor disproven": "This is the best evidence I've seen up to this time." In an example of conflicting comment in the same story, Jerry Brunton, of the Animal Health Institute, a lobbying group, found major flaws in the study: "No meat samples were available to indicate that disease-causing organisms were ever present." Another example of conflicting comment came from a *New York Times* story (#2981): "None of these links (between cancer and caffeine) has been proved to the satisfaction of scientists in general." That story also included a qualifying comment: "Other experts . . . expressed reservations concerning the implications of the new research in relating these fragile sites to cancer."

Conflicting comments also appeared in stories about pregnant women's drinking, both on ABC—"There are a lot of experts who are going to take issue with that"—and on NBC—"There is a dispute among doctors about the effect of alcohol consumption on pregnant women" (#0185 and #0190, respectively).

Total Number of Inaccuracies

As the foregoing examples suggest, some news stories may have generated multiple errors, whereas most may have been relatively error-free. In order to get a better perspective on the distribution of errors across stories, we created an index consist-

TABLE 8.1 /

Number of Inaccuracies	Number of Stories	Percent of Stories
0	3	7.1
1	7	16.7
2	11	26.2
3	12	28.6
4	6	14.3
5	2	4.8
6	1	2.4

ing of responses to six questions: substantially different, emphasis not faithful, results omitted, qualifications omitted, inaccurate headline, overgeneralizes.

Only three of the forty-two stories exhibited none of these inaccuracies, but, on the other hand, only one exhibited all six. Table 8.1 shows the distribution of stories by number of inaccuracies. Although half of the stories exhibited two or fewer inaccuracies, it ought to be remembered that seventeen of them had at least one statement coded as substantially different from one in the original source.

Earlier research on the accuracy of science reporting suggests that once the number of error categories is controlled, errors appear to occur no more often in reports about science than in news reports about other topics. Tankard and Ryan (1974), for example, reported that only 8.8 percent of their sample of science stories were perceived as error-free (the rate in the present study is 7.1 percent), compared with 40 percent and 60 percent of general news stories (as reported in other studies). However, when Pulford (1976) replicated the Tankard and Ryan study using a shorter list of errors comparable to those used in earlier accuracy studies, the number of errors identified by scientists was "quite close to the perceived error rates of the earlier general news studies" (Dunwoody and Stocking, 1986).[13]

---

[13] These accuracy studies, unlike Meyer's, included subjective judgments and did not submit the sources' complaints to journalists for their comments and further adjudication. Hence, the error rates are considerably higher than those he reports.

COMPARISONS WITH EARLIER FINDINGS

How seriously should we take the findings just reported, which are after all based on a very small and specialized sample of hazard stories?

One of the things that increases our confidence in the findings is their similarity to those of Tankard and Ryan (1974), who had a much larger sample of 193 news stories. For example, 38 percent of our stories were coded as omitting important results; 34 percent of Tankard and Ryan's stories were coded as omitting relevant information about results. Speculations were treated as fact in 18 percent of our stories and in 20 percent of Tankard & Ryan's. We coded 36 percent of our stories as overstating the generalizability of the findings, a category which included overstatement of causal implications; Tankard and Ryan coded 18 percent of their stories as overstating the generality of results and another 22 percent as overstating causal implications.

On one question, the scientists queried by Tankard and Ryan appear to have been more stringent in their coding. Headlines were coded as misleading or inaccurate 31 percent of the time in our sample, whereas Tankard and Ryan's scientists coded 31 percent of the headlines as misleading and 15 percent as inaccurate. Note, however, that these may be overlapping categories. On another question, however, having to do with information about methods, we appear to have been much more stringent than the scientists. They rated 35 percent of the stories as having omitted relevant information about methods; we coded 48 percent as making no mention of methods at all, and most of the additional stories as providing inadequate or erroneous information. Evidence from several sources suggests that scientists are themselves often careless about providing information about methods (see Weiss and Singer with Endreny, 1988, p. 240).

The most serious limitation on our findings occurs because news stories based on research reports make up a relatively small fraction of all news stories about hazards. Our sample included 1,276 hazard stories—952 in 1984 and 324 in 1960.[14] Of these, 222,

---

[14] Of these, only 781 were coded as "issue" stories; references to research were coded for these studies only (see Table 7.1).

or 17.4 percent, made some reference to research, and only 51 stories—4 percent of the total sample or 23 percent of those news stories making a reference to research—were coded as referring to published research. Another limitation of the findings is that news stories based on published research are not distributed evenly across hazard categories but come disproportionately from the category of illness stories. This is obviously not because there is no research in other areas (studies of earthquakes and studies of the effects of different toxic substances, for example, exist) but because these studies are considered less interesting, or pose greater difficulties in reporting. For both of these reasons, we cannot generalize our findings to the accuracy of hazard reporting in general.

DISCUSSION AND CONCLUSIONS

The question posed in this chapter was, How accurate is mass media reporting in hazard stories based on research reports in more specialized media of communication?

Two-fifths of the news stories we coded had one or more statements which were substantially different from statements in the original research report. This does not include the one research report we could not locate at all because the reference in the news story was incorrect. Because no comparable coding category existed in the Tankard and Ryan study, we cannot compare our results with those obtained when scientists themselves are doing the coding. But the general conclusion that has been drawn from Tankard and Ryan is that errors of omission are much more frequent than errors of commission in the reporting of science news. Our own study suggests that errors of commission also occur in a substantial number of cases.

The large number of stories containing substantially inaccurate statements is cause for concern. These statements are not matters of judgment, whether to leave something out or to put it in, nor are they attributable to ambiguous or nonexistent sources. The reports exist in written form. Nor, finally, do they appear in fly-by-night media; on the contrary, these media are the best of the mass communications world. Clearly, our findings point to a need for some remedial training, whether in journalism schools or on the job.

Many of the discrepancies observed by us, as well as by Tankard and Ryan, involve omissions of qualifying statements, details of method, and significant results. The same omissions occur in the reporting of social science (see Weiss and Singer with Endreny, 1988, part 2, chap. 3). Other changes involve shifts in emphasis, less precise wordings, and more colloquial terms.

Whether or not such omissions and alterations should be regarded as inaccurate reporting depends on how we define accuracy. For example, most existing information about risks is partial and contingent. Beliefs about whether or not a particular substance poses a hazard to humans, and how much of a hazard it poses, are based on assumptions, research findings, statistical calculations and extrapolations (sometimes from doses far higher than those likely to be received by humans, sometimes from animals that may provide only imperfect models for what happens to humans). If readers and viewers are not made aware of these contingencies, if mass media accounts do not reflect limitations in the data or the research methods used, and if conflicting findings are presented without interpretation or evaluation, then flaws exist in the communication process, whether we call these flaws inaccuracies or give them some other name.

What is particularly troubling is the suggestion in our data that omissions and alterations are more likely to occur in bylined stories than anonymous ones. It is troubling because it underlines the existence of different standards for journalists and scientists, not simply carelessness on the part of reporters protected by anonymity. On the other hand, the fact that the wire-service stories were found to contain the fewest number of substantively different statements is cause for comfort, since these stories are distributed more widely than those by individual journalists.

Science in the popular press is livelier and easier to read than science in the scholarly journals. It is also simpler, sharper, and less ambiguous than science in those journals; and science in the scholarly journals is already simpler, sharper, and much less messy than the science that takes place in the laboratory or in the field. Without a great deal of complex and difficult research, we cannot know the consequences of the sharpening and leveling[15] that of necessity takes place in the popular press. But we can speculate that science and scientists come across as more authoritative than they really are; that scientific findings are regarded with more confidence than may be warranted; that, therefore, when a disconfirming finding comes along, it may undermine the credibility of the whole structure; and that confidence in the press, as well as in science, may suffer as a result.

Developments in mass communication point to even greater constrictions in the future on the amount of space or time that can be devoted to any one news story. Thus, the tendencies toward omission that we have identified are likely to increase in the future, and so are whatever consequences they bring in their wake.

---

[15] The terms come from a classic study of the psychology of rumor, by Allport and Postman (1945), and seem to describe some of the changes that occur when a scholarly report is transformed into a news story. This does not imply that journalists are rumor-mongers. It simply suggests that the same psychological principles that underlie the transmission of rumor also serve to describe the transmission of other kinds of information. "Sharpening" is defined as "the selective perception, retention, and reporting of a limited number of details from a larger context." "Leveling" refers to the tendency to shorten material that is repeated: "Whenever verbal material is transmitted among a group of people whether as rumor, legend, or history, change will be in the direction of greater brevity and conciseness." There is an obvious relationship between sharpening and leveling; as some details are omitted, others inevitably become sharper, clearer, more important, and more memorable.

9 / Looking Back and Looking Forward

Whether we like it or not, most of the information we have about risks comes to us by way of the mass media. But it does not, for the most part, come as explicit reporting about risk. In fact, a search through the 1990 *New York Times Index* and the 1990 *Vanderbilt Television Index* turned up not a single entry under the heading of "risk." Instead, most of what we have in this book construed as reporting about hazards and their associated risks comes in the guise of news and feature stories about accidents, illnesses, natural disasters, and scientific breakthroughs.

Willy nilly, such reporting communicates risk information to consumers of the mass media and to the friends with whom they discuss what they have heard or read (Atkin, 1972; Robinson and Levy, 1986). Such information is communicated not only by what is selected for coverage and what is not, but also by how it is covered—where the story is placed, how much space or time is devoted to it, whether it is accompanied by visuals or not. All this, of course, is quite apart from the question of whether or not explicit risk-related information is included in the story, and if so, of what kind.

WHAT KINDS OF HAZARDS DO THE MEDIA REPORT?

What is it, then, that the average reader or viewer would learn from the way hazards and their associated risks are selected and presented by the media in our sample?

First, readers and viewers would learn that what is defined as a hazard changes over time. For example, in 1960, most stories about nuclear energy emphasized benefits rather than costs; by 1984, the proportions had reversed. In the 1960s, prior to the U.S. Supreme Court ruling on abortion, stories about abortion emphasized the risks of illegal abortions to the mother; in 1984, stories about abortion emphasized the risks of legal abortions for the fetus.

Second, though the hazard definitions appearing in the mass media may change, the media in all likelihood do not initiate the changes. For example, during our media-monitoring period, stories about the space shuttle were numerous but made no mention of associated risks at all; after the *Challenger* exploded, this practice underwent significant change. Or, to take another example, stories about nuclear war rarely mentioned associated risks. Rubin and Cummings (1989) chide the media for having missed many opportunities to raise issues surrounding nuclear war for public debate. But their failure to do so simply emphasizes that the media are essentially reactive. Their definitions and selections of hazards for coverage are ordinarily shaped by sources other than the media themselves.

Third, a direct comparison between hazards as topics of news stories and as causes of death shows essentially no relationship between the two. But the correlation between the number of stories about each hazard in 1960 and in 1984 is substantial as well as significant: with outliers excluded, the Spearman rank correlation coefficient between the two distributions is .81; the Pearson product-moment correlation is .94. Thus, what is newsworthy did not change very much over a period of 24 years. But what is newsworthy does not correspond very well with the distribution of hazards in the real world, as measured by mortality figures. Why not? Because, as it turns out, the media tend to feature what the *Statistical Abstract of the United States* calls "catastrophic" accidents— accidents in which five or more people are killed simultaneously.

Such accidents rank near or at the top in terms of media attention, even though with one exception, automobile accidents, they do not result in a large number of deaths per year. Thus, media definitions of risk are based on the drama of the single hazardous event, not on the cumulatively greater but less spectacular risks reflected in annual mortality figures.

We formulated a number of hypotheses about the characteristics of hazards that would be attended to by the media. First, we predicted that stories about hazards with associated deaths or injuries would be longer and featured more prominently than stories about hazards without associated deaths or injuries. This hypothesis was supported both in 1960 and in 1984. Second, we hypothesized that stories about new hazards, whether classified as such by the journalists or by us, would be longer and featured more prominently than other hazards. This hypothesis, too, was supported, and as we note in Chapter 3, this bias in favor of the new and the immediate may limit coverage of chronic hazards such as illness, air or water pollution, poverty, and hazardous working conditions, unless some dramatic happening makes them suddenly "news."

Third, we predicted that the media would attend disproportionately to hazards affecting the more affluent and powerful members of society. The lack of an objective yardstick is particularly troublesome in trying to evaluate this hypothesis. Without knowing more about the number of hazards actually affecting each group, it is difficult to say whether coverage is too much or not enough. The evidence we were able to bring to bear on this hypothesis is mixed. Relatively few stories in either year, and fewer in 1960 than in 1984, mentioned such social categories as race, gender, class, and age. But the majority of stories mentioning such categories were about the less affluent and the less powerful: blacks, women, poor people, and the elderly. Nevertheless, we conclude that the small number of stories (N = 3 in 1960 and 62 in 1984) dealing explicitly with hazards of blacks, women, the elderly, or the poor is evidence of bias—that is, a disproportionate lack of attention. On the other hand, those stories that do deal explicitly with hazards affecting one or more of these groups are not shorter than other stories; on the contrary, they are longer.

Fourth, we expected that various specialized media would attend disproportionately to the hazards of their particular audience (e.g., blacks or women), but we found no evidence for this in the small sample of specialized media we examined. Magazines and newspapers aimed at black audiences do not appear to attend disproportionately to the risks of blacks, nor do magazines aimed at women attend disproportionately to hazards affecting women. However, because of the small number of specialized media we looked at, and the short sampling period, our evidence for this hypothesis is limited.

Finally, we predicted that geographic location would affect the amount of coverage received by a hazard, with stories about countries close to the United States, geographically and culturally, receiving more coverage than warranted by the number of deaths associated with the hazardous event, and countries geographically and culturally distant receiving fewer (see Adams, 1985; Gaddy and Tanjong, 1985). The evidence for this proposition is meager, however. News about hazards in the United States is indeed given disproportionate attention in the U.S. press, but there are no consistent biases in favor of other parts of the world. Furthermore, contrary to what is predicted by the hypothesis, in the coverage of natural disasters there is no statistically significant interaction effect on story length between geographic location and number of deaths.

WHAT KIND OF INFORMATION DO THE MEDIA COMMUNICATE ABOUT RISK?

So far, we have been concerned with principles of selection and definition. But what kind of information is presented by the media about those hazards they choose to feature?

The first thing to note is that the media generally do not report on hazards and associated risks. They report on specific instances of a hazard (e.g., a flood, a plane crash, the pollution of a town's water supply) that produce or are accompanied by specific harms: so many dead, so many hurt, so many houses destroyed. From such scenarios we have abstracted, for purposes of this research, concepts of hazard and risk, benefit and cost. But these abstract concepts are not what journalism is about.

There is an inherent conflict between what social scientists and others call risk communication and the business of news. To communicate information about hazards and risks in a way calculated to foster rational decision making means to provide detailed and precise information about immediate and long-term consequences, to weigh the costs and benefits of a hazard and its alternatives for the individual and for society, and to discuss the issues, moral and economic, that inhere in hazardous processes and events.[1]

But reporting about hazards, as we have seen, is ordinarily reporting about events rather than issues, about immediate consequences rather than long-term considerations, about harms rather than risks. Precise information about risks is often unavailable and is rarely presented. Alternatives are almost never considered in a story about a particular hazard, and when they are, their risks and benefits are often not. Moral or ethical issues are generally absent from news stories about hazards, and even economic issues are for the most part ignored.

The hazard category with perhaps the closest fit between the definitions employed by the media and by risk researchers is that of materials hazards (e.g., pesticides, nuclear radiation, radon, alcohol), and so one might expect that reporting practices and researchers' expectations would mesh most closely there. But that is not the case. Reporters are no more likely to provide risk information in connection with materials hazards than they are for any other hazard category.

If these omissions were errors on the part of journalists, there would be grounds for optimism. But for the most part they are not. The most accurate reporting in the world would not necessarily include any of the details mentioned in the paragraph above. Nothing in the rules of journalism says that the reporter must, in addition to describing an industrial accident, also inform readers about the likelihood of such an event occurring again, or about the risks posed by the industry in general, or about alternatives and their benefits and costs. It is true that "enterprise" journalism might deal with any or all of these issues, but enterprise journalism is likely to remain a minor part of the journalistic enterprise.

---

[1] Beyond this core information, Dunwoody (1991) talks about what details a "useful" article should contain to enable a concerned citizen to follow through with a reasonable rather than a Herculean effort.

HOW ACCURATE IS THE INFORMATION COMMUNICATED?

A broad definition of accuracy might include all of the components discussed in the section above, insisting that in order to be accurate, news stories about a hazard should also be comprehensive: they should include details such as the likelihood of its occurrence; the annual mortality associated with it, if it occurs; the spatial extent of the hazard; whether or not it is likely to affect succeeding generations; and whether or not alternatives to the hazard are safer or less safe than the one under consideration.

If this were the standard of accuracy, then, as we have seen, most hazard reporting would have to be considered inaccurate. Instead, however, we adopted a much less stringent standard, one against which we were able to test only a subset of all hazard stories.

In brief, we identified all those news or feature stories in our sample that referred to a research report and cited a published source for that report. Earlier studies of accuracy in science reporting, relying mainly on evaluations of accuracy by scientist sources, had suggested that the errors in news stories about science were largely errors of omission rather than commission (e.g., Tankard and Ryan, 1974). Although we found such errors as well, we also found a substantial number of errors of commission— statements in the news story that were substantively different from those in the original report. In addition, two (out of forty-four) research reports could not be located at all, because the reference to a source in the news story was incorrect.

Unlike the issue of detail and breadth in hazard reporting, which we suggested above was likely to remain a problem from the perspective of risk communicators and social scientists, the narrow question of accuracy we have posed above ought to be susceptible to improvement. Perhaps what is needed is a joint effort by journalists and scientists, sitting around a table with some actual science reports and the news stories based on them, to arrive at a working guide for what, at a minimum, every such news story should contain.

But the question of accuracy, as we have posed it, is only the tip of the iceberg. Much more frequent than a news report on an isolated study is the incorporation of many different research findings into a news story about a particular hazard (e.g., radon). In that situation, reporters must present not the results of one study but the conclusions of a number of scientists working in a given area. And the fact is that scientists often disagree, from whether or not the "big bang" theory can explain the origin of the universe, to whether or not electromagnetic fields are capable of causing cancer, to how much of a threat radon in homes really is. Under these circumstances, what does accurate reporting demand?

The typical American practice of "objective" journalism consists of presenting both (or more than two) divergent points of view on the issue.[2] Whether that is accurate reporting or not depends on whether the different positions are really equally compelling, or whether the weight of evidence clearly favors one side or the other. Unfortunately, this is information that the reader or viewer is rarely made privy to. In a speech in which John Kemeny, then president of Dartmouth College and chairman of the president's commission investigating the Three Mile Island accident, talked about his experiences on the commission, Kemeny noted that "the two sides of every scientific controversy do not necessarily deserve equal space." He said he expected one day to read in the morning paper the following story: "Three scientists by the names of Galileo, Newton, and Einstein have concluded that the earth is round. However, the *New York Times* has learned authoritatively that Professor John Doe has exclusive evidence that the earth is flat."[3]

The even-handed model of reporting on political opinions or issue positions is not necessarily a good one for the reporting of risk. The reader or viewer needs an appraisal of the evidence, by a knowledgeable source: Which, if any, side does it favor? Is it too early to tell? When is better evidence likely to become available? Internist and television reporter Dr. Timothy Johnson says, "I think of myself as an interpreter. I try to look at stories and put

[2]Schiller (1981) notes that the links between the ideals of science and the norm of objectivity in journalism were formed in the mid-nineteenth century, when they were seen as necessary to avoid factionalism in an increasingly diverse society. See also Schudson (1978).
[3]Quoted in Robert W. Lundeen, "The Media and Industry: Two Different Worlds," speech given at the University of Missouri, October 1983.

them in perspective . . . to say 'This is what it means.' " Without doing that, Johnson says, "reporters can't separate the wheat from the chaff."[4] Johnson, himself a physician, reports on medical news. But separating the wheat from the chaff often requires more detailed knowledge of a subject than most journalists can reasonably be expected to have. Hence, the issue of accuracy and balance is likely to remain a troublesome one in risk reporting.

WHO IS HELD ACCOUNTABLE FOR THE HAZARD?

In this study we distinguished two kinds of accountability: first, blame for the occurrence of a hazard; and second, responsibility for its prevention. Media attributions of accountability were much more frequent in the second, preventive sense than in the first. Further, those agents responsible for preventive action against a hazard were not necessarily the same ones as those blamed for its occurrence.

At least half of the stories we analyzed made no attributions of blame at all, either because responsibility was taken for granted, or because the issue of blame did not arise. For example, stories about natural hazards were particularly unlikely to include explicit attributions of blame. We noted no differences in this tendency either over time or between media.

We began by asking whether there were any patterns in the assignment of blame for the occurrence of a hazard, and it soon became clear that the pattern varied according to the type of hazard involved. Victims, for example, tended to be held accountable in the case of activities involving benefits and costs, but not in the case of other hazards.[5] This tendency, too, showed no changes over time.

---

[4]Quoted in Maryann Haggerty and Charles D. Bankhead, "Medicine and the Media," *Medicial World News*, June 25, 1984. Johnson's comment about separating the wheat from the chaff echoes that of Meyer, commenting on the "even-handed" reporting of conflicting poll results: "If the highly educated staff of a metropolitan newspaper cannot interpret such a discrepancy [in poll results], how can the poor reader be expected to do it?" (Quoted in Weiss and Singer with Endreny, 1988, p. 252.)

[5]Although relatively few (12 percent in 1984, and 18 percent in 1960) stories about illness ascribed any blame or responsibility at all, 5 out of 12 of those stories assigning any blame at all blamed the victim.

We had hypothesized that victims would tend to be blamed in stories about hazards involving vested interests, as in smoking and alcohol consumption. Our analysis made it clear, however, that the pattern of blaming victims was much more general, extending to all activities that could be construed as voluntary. In a sense, then, the more interesting question to ask is how some activities come to be construed as voluntary, others as involuntary. The ongoing debate about whether or not alcoholism is an illness, and the extent to which heredity is responsible for its expression, is a case in point, but laws, regulation, and advertisements can also be seen as circumscribing the extent to which activities are undertaken voluntarily.

Recent interest in the study of public responses to radon (e.g., Sandman, Weinstein, and Klotz, 1987) has turned up an apparently paradoxical finding: risks tend to be perceived as more serious when there is someone to blame (see also Baum, Fleming, and Davidson, 1983). Radon resulting from natural deposits of radioactive rock tends to be ignored by the public, whereas radon resulting from industrial waste disposal has led to organized public demands for cleaning up the offending source. It is unclear to what extent the media would or could counteract this tendency, which from the point of view of scientists assessing the relative risks of the two sources of radon is misplaced (Sandman, Weinstein, and Klotz, 1987, citing Baum, Fleming, and Davidson, 1983).

We found no differences between media in their attributions of blame to different targets. But because reporting on risk is event-centered, they all tend to make what Fischhoff has called the fundamental attribution error: the tendency to attribute too much responsibility to individual actors, including individual corporations, and too little to the social and environmental constraints within which they act.

THE POLITICS OF RISK REPORTING

The literature on risk reporting appears to us to reflect two distinct perspectives, which correspond to the underying paradigms of sociology itself. There is, on the one hand, what we would call a consensus perspective and, on the other, a conflict perspective. Diagnoses of the ills of risk reporting vary depending on which of these two perspectives inform the analysis.

Those who take an essentially consensual view of society criticize reporters for neglecting to put risks in perspective, for failing to report on benefits, for showing the one person (out of, say, 100,000) who is harmed by a drug's side effects, for choosing the worst-case end of a range of possible hazard effects as the story's lead.

The remedies proposed by this group of critics likewise reflect a consensual view of social institutions, stressing primarily better communication and cooperation between scientists and journalists. For example, the Institute for Health Policy Analysis of Georgetown University has sponsored a number of workshops on health-risk reporting, and the 1984 "Workshop Summary Report," prepared by Stephen Klaidman, concludes: "Suggestions (for improving risk reporting) included one from (Sam) Gorovitz that journalists be taught some cognitive psychology to give them a better understanding of how people use information to reach conclusions; one from Howard Lewis, former director of public affairs for the National Academy of Sciences, that scientists volunteer their expertise, especially in local emergency situations (he cited the case of Three Mile Island, where highly qualified local experts had important information but did not notify the press or local officials); and one from (Barbara) Culliton that research institutions should hold seminars for journalists to keep them up to date and to help them understand the nuances of the latest developments in science." Reading the recommendations of the workshop organizers and participants, one is reminded of the proposals of the human relations school of industrial psychology in the forties and fifties, which sought to minimize conflict between management and labor by bringing representatives of both to workshops, roundtables, and sensitivity groups designed to improve communication and interpersonal relations between them (see Haire, 1954, esp. 1121).

Among those subscribing to a conflict rather than consensual model of social processes, cooperation between journalists and scientists is viewed with suspicion rather than as a remedy. Nelkin, whose many publications (e.g., 1984, 1985, 1985a, 1987, 1988) place her in this second group, for example, would rather see a more independent, well-qualified corps of journalists who systematically challenge the supposedly neutral pronouncements of "objective" scientists on issues related to risk. Or, as Wilkins and Patterson (1987:90) put it, "Risk communication is no different than communication about any other form of politics: it's a story of who gets what and at what cost. . . . Once reporters and editors frame the story as something other than an event, covering risk is not so different from covering pork barrel legislation or some forms of investigative journalism." Urging reporters to cover "normal accidents" as a series of interlocking decisions rather than as discrete events and to include more precise reporting of the statistical nature of risk and its cultural context, Wilkins and Patterson quote from Perrow's analysis of how the accident at Chernobyl came about (1986:356):

> Catastrophes are possible where community and regional interests are not mobilized or when they are over-ridden by national policy; when the economic costs of the disaster can be displaced from the private or governmental organization in charge to the rest of society; and when supranational goals, such as the economic health of an industry deemed vital or the control of outer space, are served.

In this view, the appropriate role of the press is to mobilize countervailing interests, as in the case of Love Canal or the preservative Alar, not to alleviate the public's concern by putting such risks in perspective. As Nelkin (1988a:17–18) puts it:

> The coverage of the Rhine River chemical spill alerted the public throughout Europe to the danger of chemical spills in common waters. . . . By their selection of newsworthy events, journalists identify pressing policy issues. By their focus on controversial issues, they stimulate demands for accountability. By their use of images they help to create the judgmental biases that underlie public policy. The real power of the press, claimed Harold Laski, comes from "its ability to surround facts by an environment of suggestions which, often half consciously, seeks its way into the mind of the reader and forms his premises for him." (Quoted from Laski (1984) in Nelkin, 1988a)

Those seeking to form the reader's "premises for him" are not, however, necessarily limited to any one point of view about the hazards and risks of modern life. In fact, one of the most disturbing trends in mass communication is the increasing manipulation of media content, including the content of the news, in a deliberate attempt to mold public opinion and even behavior. Others have commented on the blurring of distinctions between news and entertainment on television, for example in so-called recreations of events at which no reporter or camera crew was present, but which the television producer knows or assumes to have occurred, in order to lend verisimilitude to a news story.[6] In the short run, the exchange value of the image—"one picture is worth a thousand words"—is likely to enhance the story's credibility, even when it is false. In the long run, the practice is likely to erode further the confidence the public has in the media.[7]

One area in which the issue of manipulation arises with special force is that of public-health campaigns. Although the goals of these campaigns may be laudable—for example, to reduce drunk driving—the means being advocated by some public-health communication experts are raising questions among media professionals and others concerned about issues of censorship and propaganda. The most disputed recommendations involve using staged events, distributing news releases that mimic the conventions of television news, and inserting public-health messages into the content of entertainment programming in order to bypass people's defenses against the influence attempts of clearly identified public service advertisements (see, e.g., Winston and DeJong, 1990). While proponents of such deliberate techniques can point to the subtle and effective influencing of public attitudes and values that already occurs, even without deliberate intent, in entertainment programming,[8] we question whether the presumed

[6]See, for example, Walter Goodman, "When Pictures Dictate the News," *New York Times*, November 19, 1989, sec. 2, p. 32.

[7]The question of media credibility received a great deal of attention and debate in 1986 (see, for example, American Society of Newspaper Editors, 1986; Whitney, 1986; Times-Mirror Company, January 1986 and September 1986; Lipset and Schneider, 1987). Although different measures lead to somewhat different conclusions, Lipset and Schneider's comparative analysis suggests that the "leaders" of the press are not perceived with a great deal of confidence. The standing of the press relative to other institutions, however, has not shown a decline (Lipset and Schneider, 1987:48–49).

[8]For example, the association of smoking and drinking with elegance, affluence, and good health in such programs. See also Krugman (1965) and Gerbner et al. (1980, 1982).

life-style gains from the new techniques are worth the costs in terms of media credibility and trust. And it is worth repeating that the focus of such campaigns is, once again, the individual—individual smokers, not R. J. Reynolds; designated drivers instead of a ban on liquor advertisements. Thus, these proposed campaigns insidiously reinforce the notions of individual responsibility and individual blame for what may, more appropriately, be regarded as largely socially determined behavior.

WHO SETS THE MEDIA'S AGENDA?

Given the ideological and policy implications of reporting on hazards and risk, it is worth asking who sets the agenda for the media. The answers are only gradually beginning to emerge from diverse research. Rogers and Dearing (1988), for example, refer to it as "an obviously important question, but one that has virtually been ignored by mass communication researchers" (p. 559). They go on to note that, in their struggle to give meaning to the flow of news coming to them each day, editors and other decision makers frequently turn to other media "to help determine news priorities. The *New York Times* is considered particularly important in setting the daily news agenda for other mass media in the U.S.," but other "elite" media are frequently included among agenda setters, especially for specific areas (e.g., the *Washington Post* for national news, the *Wall Street Journal* for business news), and the wire services are repeatedly acknowledged as a vital factor in inter-media influence. Since 1985 there has been some attention devoted to the question of inter-media influence (e.g., Turk, 1989; Reese and Daniellian, 1989; Abbott and Brassfield, 1989; and Harmon, 1989).

McCombs (1989) broadens the list of agenda setters for the media to include the federal government, in particular the White House, and notes that coverage of pollution doubled following President Richard Nixon's emphasis on the topic in his 1970 "State of the Union" address. A searching examination by Gladwell (1986) of how and why the drug-abuse story suddenly became news in 1986, when statistics showed no particular increase in usage, likewise identified the White House, Congress, and a number of elite media as the key actors: Between November 17, 1985 and October 1, 1986, "the major media—the *New York Times,* the *Washington Post,* the *Los Angeles Times,* the wire services, *Time, Newsweek,* and *U.S. News and World Report*—had among them carried more than a thousand stories in which crack and other drugs figured prominently, coverage feeding coverage, stories of addiction and squalor multiplying across the land."[9]

So far, of course, we have been talking about agenda setting in general, not about agenda setting in the specific area of risk reporting. But although we lack hard evidence, we believe that risk reporting does not differ very much from reporting in general. Like other reporters, those who cover materials hazards or health hazards are dependent on sources associated with the relevant institutions: the medical and scientific journals and the scientists who write for them, the regulatory agencies, the spokespersons for industries and hospitals.[10] News values are no different in the area of risk reporting than they are in any other area. And the agenda for reporting on risk is, we suspect, set in the same ways as it is for other topics. Future study is clearly needed on the processes by which such agenda setting actually occurs.

TURNABOUT ON ATTITUDES TOWARD RISK?

We noted in Chapter 5 that we could find no evidence of increasing aversion to risk on the part of the media in the last twenty-four years. On the contrary, we found some very slight tendency in the reverse direction. Hazard stories in 1984 gave somewhat more attention to benefits than they had in 1960, and they were also somewhat more likely to include a discussion of alternatives to the hazard and to reject the alternative in favor of the hazard itself. These are all small shifts, to be sure, and they may involve reporting on different hazards rather than a changing view of specific hazards. Still, they may be indicative of a subtle change in the social climate pertaining to the acceptance of risk.

A number of stories appearing in the *New York Times* since the end of our intensive media monitoring period also suggest the possibility of such a shift. A two-part series by Peter Passell, on May 8 and May 9, 1989 ("The American Sense of Peril: A Stifling

---

[9]See also Reese and Daniellian (1989).
[10]See, for example, Stallings (1990).

Cost of Modern Life," and "Making a Risky Life Bearable: Better Data, Clearer Choices"), for example, poses the tradeoffs in its first two paragraphs:

> Is the slight risk of contracting cancer from Alar too high a price to pay for crisper apples? Is the dramatic increase in milk production available through genetically engineered growth hormones worth the unknown risk to children's health? . . . While there is little statistical evidence that the hazards of daily life are on the rise, a wide range of academic and business experts believe that Americans' perception of increased peril is stifling technology, wasting billions of dollars and, ironically, making it more difficult to contain the most serious risks.

Passell goes on, in the second article, to discuss such issues as allowing medical patients formally to give up the right to punitive damages in return for lower fees, substituting expert judgments for jury awards in cases of product liability, and compensating individuals or communities for exceptional exposure to risk. No such articles appeared in the press we monitored in 1984 or 1960.

We noted earlier that the media are reactive, not only in the sense of reporting on events that have already occurred rather than anticipating future trends, but also in the sense that they rarely, if ever, structure the terms of the debate about issues. Instead, they adopt the frames provided by dominant social institutions. The eighties in the United States, beginning with the presidency of Ronald Reagan and continuing with that of George Bush, came to symbolize the retrenchment of government in favor of increasingly unregulated private activity—a development spurred, perhaps, by decades of increasing regulation and government expansion. At the same time, the economic situation of the country consistently declined. Increasing media emphasis on the benefits of risky activities instead of their costs, and on the considerable costs of reducing these risks, may well reflect both of these social trends.

What is needed to complement this study of reporting practices is a study of public perceptions of risk and of the extent to which these are, indeed, shaped by the media. Psychologists such as Fischhoff and Slovic, and Kahneman and Tversky, have illuminated many of the determinants of public sentiments about hazards and their associated risks. These determinants include both characteristics of the hazard itself (e.g., the extent to which exposure to it is perceived to be voluntary, whether or not the risks associated with it are seen as catastrophic) and aspects of the way the risks are presented (e.g., people are less willing to expose themselves to a risk of "dying" than to a risk of "surviving," or to a risk of "losing" rather than "winning," even when the probabilities of surviving or winning are identical under the two formulations). We have, in this study, documented media practices relevant to many of these points. But how media presentations interact with apparently variable individual predispositions, and to what extent such predispositions are themselves socially shaped, either by the media or by other societal processes, remains very much an open question.

References

Abbott, E. A., and L. T. Brassfield. "Comparing Decisions on Releases by TV and Newspaper Gatekeepers." *Journalism Quarterly* 66 (1989): 853–857.

Adams, W. C. "Whose Lives Count? TV Coverage of Natural Disasters." *Journal of Communication* 36(2) (1986): 113–122.

Allport, G., and L. Postman. "The Psychology of Rumor." In E. E. Maccoby et al., *Readings in Social Psychology*, 3d ed. New York: Holt, Rinehart and Winston, 1958.

Altheide, D. L. *Creating Reality*. Beverly Hills, CA: Sage, 1976.

———. *Media Power*. Beverly Hills, CA: Sage, 1985.

Altman, L. "The Press and AIDS." *Bulletin of The New York Academy of Medicine* 64(6) (1988): 520–528.

American Society of Newspaper Editors. "Newspaper Credibility," April 1986.

Apostle, R., C. Y. Glock, T. Piazza, and M. Suelzle. *The Anatomy of Racial Attitudes.* Berkeley and Los Angeles: University of California Press, 1983.

Atkin, C. K. "Anticipated Communication and Mass Media Information-Seeking." *Public Opinion Quarterly* 36 (1972): 188–199.

Barnhurst, K. J. "The Great American Newspaper." *The American Scholar* 60 (1991): 106–112.

———, and J. C. Nerone. "Design Trends in U.S. Front Pages, 1885–1985." *Journalism Quarterly* 68 (1991): 796–804.

Barton, A. H. *Communities in Disaster*. Garden City, NY: Doubleday, 1969, 1970.

Baum, A., R. Fleming, and L. M. Davidson. "National Disaster and Technological Catastrophe." *Environment and Behavior* 15(3) (1983): 333–354.

Becker, L. B. "The Mass Media and Citizen Assessment of Issue Importance: A

Reflection on Agenda-Setting Research." In D. C. Whitney, E. Wartella, and S. Windahl, eds. *Mass Communication Review Yearbook 3*, pp. 521–536. Beverly Hills, CA: Sage, 1982.

Borman, S. C. "Communication Accuracy in Magazine Science Reporting." *Journalism Quarterly* 55 (1978): 345–346.

Boyer, P. "Famine in Ethiopia." *Washington Journalism Review* 7 (January 1985): 18–21.

Bradburn, N. M., and C. Miles. "Vague Quantifiers." *Public Opinion Quarterly* 43 (1979): 92–101.

Bridges, J. A. "News Use on the Front Pages of the American Daily." *Journalism Quarterly* 66 (Summer 1989): 332–337.

Broberg, K. "Scientists' Stopping Behavior as Indicators of Writers' Skill." *Journalism Quarterly* 50 (1973): 763–767.

Cantril, H. *The Invasion from Mars: A Study in the Psychology of Panic.* Princeton, NJ: Princeton University Press, 1940.

Carson, R. *Silent Spring.* Boston, MA: Houghton Mifflin, 1962.

Cohen, B. C. *The Press, the Public and Foreign Policy.* Princeton, NJ: Princeton University Press, 1963.

Cole, J. R. "Dietary Cholesterol and Heart Disease: The Construction of a Medical Fact." In H. J. O'Gorman, ed. *Surveying Social Life*, pp. 437–466. Middletown, CT: Wesleyan University Press, 1987.

Combs, B., and P. Slovic. "Newspaper Coverage of Causes of Death." *Journalism Quarterly* 56 (1979): 837–843.

Cook, F. L. "The Role of Social Science Knowledge in Moving Issues Onto and Off Policy Agendas: A Case Study." Paper presented at Conference on Knowledge Use, Pittsburgh, PA, March 18–20, 1981.

Cook, T. D., D. A. Kendzierski, and S. V. Thomas. "The Implicit Assumptions of Television Research: An Analysis of the 1982 NIMH Report on *Television and Behavior*." *Public Opinion Quarterly* 47 (1983): 161–201.

Desai, M. "Storytelling and Formalism in Economics: The Instance of Famine." *International Social Science Journal* 39 (August 1987): 387–400.

Diamond, E. "New Wrinkles on the Permanent Press." *Public Opinion* 7 (April/May 1984): 4.

Didion, J. "New York: Sentimental Journeys." *New York Review of Books* 38 (Jan. 17, 1991): 45–56.

Douglas, M., and A. Wildavsky. *Risk and Culture.* Berkeley, CA: University of California Press, 1982.

Dunwoody, S. "Inclusion of 'Useful' Detail in Newspaper Coverage of High-Level Nuclear Waste Siting Controversy." *Journalism Quarterly* 68 (1991): 1.

———, and S. M. Friedman. "Panel Discussion: What Makes a Good Science Story?" In S. M. Friedman, S. Dunwoody, and C. L. Rogers, eds. *Scientists and Journalists.* New York: Free Press, 1986.

———, and H. S. Stocking. "Social Scientists and Journalists." In E. A. Rubinstein and J. Brown, eds. *The Media, Social Science, and Social Policy for Children.* Norwood, NJ: Ablex, 1985.

Epstein, E. J. *News from Nowhere.* New York: Random House, 1973.

Erbring, L., E. N. Goldenberg, and A. H. Miller. "Front-Page News and Real World Cues: A New Look at Agenda-Setting by the Media." *American Journal of Political Science* 24 (1980): 16–49.

Eyal, C. H. "The Roles of Newspapers and Television in Agenda Setting." In G. C. Wilhoit and H. de Bock, eds. *Mass Communication Review Yearbook 2.* Beverly Hills, CA: Sage, 1981.

———, J. P. Winter, and W. F. DeGeorge. "The Concept of Time Frame in Agenda Setting." In G. C. Wilhoit and H. de Bock, eds. *Mass Communication Review Yearbook 2.* Beverly Hills, CA: Sage, 1981.

Fischhoff, B. "Behavioral Aspects of Cost-Benefit Analysis." In G. T. Goodman and W. D. Rowe, eds. *Energy Risk Management,* pp. 269–283. New York: Academic Press, 1979.

———. "Managing Risk Perceptions." *Issues in Science and Technology* 11 (1985): 83–96.

Friedman, S. M. "A Case of Benign Neglect: Coverage of Three Mile Island Before the Accident." In S. M. Friedman, S. Dunwoody, and C. L. Rogers, eds. *Scientists and Journalists.* New York: Free Press, 1986.

———. "Radiation Risk Reporting: How Well Is the Press Doing Its Job?" *USA Today,* July 1991, pp. 79–81.

Freimuth, V. S., and J. P. Van Nevel. "Reaching the Public: The Asbestos Awareness Campaign." *Journal of Communication* 31(2) (1981): 155–167.

Funkhouser, G. R. "The Issues of the Sixties: An Exploratory Study in the Dynamics of Public Opinion." *Public Opinion Quarterly* 37 (1973): 62–75.

Gaddy, G. D., and E. Tanjong. "Earthquake Coverage by the Western Press." *Journal of Communication* 36(2) (1986): 105–112.

Gale, R. P. "Calculating Risk: Radiation and Chernobyl." *Journal of Communication* 37(3) (1987): 68–73.

Gans, H. *Deciding What's News.* New York: Pantheon, 1979.

Gerbner, G., and L. Gross. "Living with Television: The Violence Profile. *Journal of Communication* 26 (1976): 173–179.

Gerbner, G., et al. "Violence Profile No. 8: The Highlights." *Journal of Communication* 27 (1977): 171–180.

———. "The 'Mainstreaming' of America: Violence Profile No. 11." *Journal of Communication* 30 (1980): 10–29.

———. "Charting the Mainstream: Television's Contributions to Political Orientations." *Journal of Communication* 32 (1982): 100–127.

Gladwell, M. "A New Addiction to an Old Story." *Insight,* part 1, pp. 8–12, Oct. 27, 1986.

Glock, C. Y., and T. Piazza. "Exploring Reality Structures." In D. Anthony and T. Robbins, eds. *In Gods We Trust.* New Brunswick, NJ: Transaction Books, 1981.

Goleman, D. "New Studies Examine Sexual Guilt." *New York Times,* p. C1, Aug. 20, 1985.

Graber, D. A. "The Impact of Media Research on Public Opinion Studies." In D. C. Whitney, E. Wartella, and S. Windahl, eds. *Mass Communication Review Yearbook 3,* pp. 555–564. Beverly Hills, CA: Sage, 1982.

———. *Mass Media and American Politics.* Washington, DC: Congressional Quarterly Press, 1980.

Gusfield, J. R. *The Culture of Public Problems: Drinking-Driving and the Symbolic Order.* Berkeley, CA: University of California Press, 1981.

Harmon, M. D. "Mr. Gates Goes Electronic: The What and Why Questions in Local TV News." *Journalism Quarterly* 66 (1989): 857–863.

Heylin, M. (Editorial). *Chemical and Engineering News* 62(25) (June 18, 1984): 5.

Hirsch, P. M. "The 'Scary World' of the Nonviewer and Other Anomalies: A Reanalysis of Gerbner et al.'s Findings of Cultivation Analysis, Pt. I." *Communication Research* 7 (1980): 403–456; "On Not Learning from One's Own Mistakes: A Reanalysis . . . , Pt. II." *Communication Research* 8 (1981): 3–37.

Hohenemser, C., R. W. Kates, and P. Slovic. "The Nature of Technological Hazard." *Science* 220 (Apr. 22, 1983): 378–384.

Hughes, M. "The Fruits of Cultivation Analysis." *Public Opinion Quarterly* 44 (1980): 287–302.

Iyengar, S. "Television News and Citizens' Explanations of National Affairs." *American Political Science Review* 81 (1987): 815–831.

———, and D. R. Kinder. *News That Matters.* Chicago: University of Chicago Press, 1987.

Iyengar, S., M. D. Peters, and D. R. Kinder. "Experimental Demonstrations of the Not-So-Minimal Consequences of Television News Programs." *American Political Science Review* 76 (1982): 848–858.

Jasanoff, S. *Risk Management and Political Culture: A Comparative Study of Science in the Policy Context.* New York: Russell Sage, 1986.

Johnson, B. B., and V. T. Covello, eds. *The Social Construction of Risk.* Dordrecht, the Netherlands: D. Reidel, 1987.

Jones, E. F., J. R. Beniger, and C. F. Westoff. "Pill and IUD Discontinuation in the United States, 1970–75: The Influence of the Media." *Family Planning Perspectives* 12 (1980): 293–300.

Kahneman, D., and A. Tversky. "The Psychology of Preferences." *Scientific American* 246 (1982): 160–173.

Kasperson, R. E., et al. "The Social Amplification of Risk: A Conceptual Framework." *Risk Analysis* 8 (1988): 177–187.

Kessler, L. "Women's Magazines' Coverage of Smoking-Related Health Hazards." *Journalism Quarterly* 66 (1989): 316–323, 445.

Knopf, T. A. *Rumors, Race and Riots.* New Brunswick, NJ: Transaction Books, 1978.

Krugman, H. E. "The Impact of Television Advertising." *Public Opinion Quarterly* 29 (1965): 349–356.

Kurzman, D. *A Killing Wind.* New York: McGraw-Hill, 1987.

Landis, J. R., and G. G. Koch. "The Measurement of Observer Agreement for Categorical Data." *Biometrika* 33 (1977): 159–174.

Laski, H. *The American Democracy.* New York: Viking Press, 1984.

Lasswell, H. "The Structure and Function of Communication in Society." In L. Bryson, ed. *The Communication of Ideas.* New York: Harper and Row, 1948.

Lawless, E. W. *Technology and Social Shock.* New Brunswick, NJ: Rutgers University Press, 1977.

Lewis, D. A., and G. W. Salem. *Fear of Crime: Incivility and the Production of a Social Problem.* New Brunswick, NJ: Transaction Books, 1986.

Lichter, S. R., S. Rothman, and L. S. Lichter. *The Media Elite.* Washington, DC: Adler and Adler, 1986.

Lipset, S. M., and W. Schneider. *The Confidence Gap.* Rev. ed. Baltimore, MD: The Johns Hopkins University Press, 1987.

McCall, R. "Science and the Press." *American Psychologist* 43 (1988): 87–94.

————, and S. H. Stocking. "Between Scientists and Public." *American Psychologist* 37 (1982): 985–995.

McCombs, M. E. "Agenda-Setting." In E. Barnouw, ed. *International Encyclopedia of Communication.* New York: Oxford University Press, 1989.

————, and D. L. Shaw. "The Agenda-Setting Function of the Mass Media." *Public Opinion Quarterly* 36 (1972): 176–187.

McKean, K. "Decisions, Decisions." *Discover,* pp. 22–31, June, 1985.

MacKuen, M. J., and S. L. Coombs. *More Than News: Media Power in Public Affairs.* Beverly Hills, CA: Sage, 1981.

McNeil, B., S. Pauker, H. Sox, Jr., and A. Tversky. "On the Elicitation of Preferences for Alternative Therapies." *New England Journal of Medicine* 306 (1982): 1259–1262.

Mazur, A. "Media Coverage and Public Opinion on Scientific Controversies." *Journal of Communication* 31 (1981a): 106–115.

————. *Dynamics of Technical Controversy.* Washington, DC: Communications Press, 1981b.

————, and K. M. Waba. "The Mass Media at Love Canal and Three Mile Island." Paper presented at American Sociological Association Conference, Detroit, MI, 1983.

Meyer, P. "A Workable Measure of Auditing Accuracy in Newspapers." *Newspaper Research Journal* 10 (1988): 39–51.

Mitchell, R. C. "Polling on Nuclear Power: A Critique of the Polls after Three Mile Island." In A. H. Cantril, ed. *Polling on the Issues,* pp. 66–87. Washington, DC: Seven Locks Press, 1980.

Mutz, D. C. "Beyond Personal Influence: The Potential for Impersonal Influence in Contemporary American Politics." Paper presented at the annual conference of the American Association for Public Opinion Research, St. Petersburg, FL, May 1992.

Nader, R. *Unsafe at Any Speed: The Designed-In Dangers of the American Automobile.* New York: Grossman, 1965.

Nealey, S., W. Rankin, and D. Montano. *A Comparative Analysis of Print Media Coverage of Nuclear Power and Coal Issues.* Seattle, WA: Battelle Human Affairs Research Centers, 1978.

Nelkin, D. "Communicating the Risks and Benefits of Technology." Unpublished manuscript, 1988a.

————, ed. *The Language of Risk.* Beverly Hills, CA: Sage, 1985a.

————. *Science in the Streets.* New York: Twentieth Century Fund, 1984.

————. *Selling Science.* New York: W. H. Freeman and Co., 1987.

————. "Managing Biomedical News." *Social Research* 52 (1985): 625–646.

————. "Placing Blame for Devastating Disease." *Sociological Research* 55 (1988): 361–378.

Nickerson, A. "Gannett's Good Idea." *Columbia Journalism Review* (Mar./Apr. 1989): 12.

Page, B. I., R. Y. Shapiro, and G. R. Dempsey. "What Moves Public Opinion?" *American Political Science Review* 81 (1987): 23–44.

Page, B. I., and R. Y. Shapiro. *Fifty Years of Trends in Americans' Policy Preferences.* Chicago: University of Chicago Press, 1992.

Perrow, C. *Normal Accidents.* New York: Basic Books, 1984.

————. "Risky Systems: The Habit of Courting Disaster." *The Nation*, pp. 329, 347–56, Oct. 11, 1986.

Pfund, N., and L. Hofstadter. "Biomedical Innovation and the Press." *Journal of Communication* 32 (1981): 138–154.

Post, J. F., et al. "Reporting on Radon: The Role of Local Newspapers." Paper presented at the Association for Education in Journalism and Mass Communication Annual Meeting, Norman, OK, 1986.

Protess, D. L., and M. E. McCombs, eds. *Agenda Setting: Readings on Media, Public Opinion, and Policymaking.* Hillsdale, NJ: L. Erlbaum Associates, 1991.

Pulford, D. L. "Follow-up Study of Science News Accuracy." *Journalism Quarterly* 53 (1976): 119–121.

Rankin, W., and S. Nealy. *A Comparative Analysis of Network Television News Coverage of Nuclear Power, Coal, and Solar Stories.* Seattle, WA: Battelle Human Affairs Research Centers, 1979.

Raymond, C. A. "Risk in the Press: Conflicting Journalistic Ideologies." In Nelkin, D., ed. *The Language of Risk*, pp. 97–134. Beverly Hills, CA: Sage, 1985a.

Reese, S., and L. H. Daniellian. "Intermedia Influence and the Drug Issue: Converging on Cocaine." In P. J. Shoemaker, ed. *Communication Campaigns about Drugs: Government, the Media and the Public.* Hillsdale, NJ: L. Erlbaum Associates, 1989.

Robinson, J. P., and M. R. Levy. "Interpersonal Communication and News Comprehension." *Public Opinion Quarterly* 50 (1986): 160–175.

Rogers, E. M., and J. W. Dearing. "Agenda-Setting Research: Where Has It Been, Where Is It Going?" In J. Anderson, ed. *Communication Yearbook* 11, pp. 555–594. Newbury Park, CA: Sage, 1988.

Rosenblum, M. *Coups and Earthquakes.* New York: Harper and Row, 1981.

Rosengren, K. E., P. Arvidson, and D. Sturesson. "The Barseback 'Panic': A Radio Programme as a Negative Summary Event." *Acta Sociologica* 18 (1974): 303–321.

Roshco, B. *Newsmaking.* Chicago: University of Chicago Press, 1975.

Rubin, D. M., and C. Cummings. "Nuclear War and Its Consequences in Television News." *Journal of Communication* 39(1) (1989): 39–58.

Sandman, P. M., N. D. Weinstein, and M. L. Klotz. "Public Response to the Risk from Geological Radon." *Journal of Communication* 37(3) (1987): 93–108.

Sandman, P. M., et al. *Environmental Risk and the Press.* New Brunswick, NJ: Transaction Books, 1987.

Scanlon, T. J., R. Luukko, and G. Morton. "Media Coverage of Crises: Better than Reported, Worse than Necessary." *Journalism Quarterly* 55 (1978): 68–72.

Schiller, D. *Objectivity and the News.* Philadelphia: University of Pennsylvania Press, 1981.

Schribman, D. "Calculating the Odds on Risk Assessment." *New York Times*, p. E9, Jan. 2, 1983.

Schudson, M. *Discovering the News: A Social History of American Newspapers.* New York: Basic Books, 1978.

Shapiro, S., "Caution: This Story Has Not Been Fact Checked. Read at Your Own Risk." New York: Columbia University, Freedom Forum Media Studies Center, Working Paper, 1989.

Shaver, K. G. *The Attribution of Blame: Causality, Responsibility, and Blameworthiness.* New York: Springer-Verlag, 1985.

Singer, E., and J. Ludwig. "South Africa's Press Ban and U.S. Public Opinion." *Public Opinion Quarterly* 51 (1987): 315–334.

Singer, E., T. F. Rogers, and M. B. Glassman. "Public Opinion about AIDS before and after the U.S. Government Information Campaign of 1988." *Public Opinion Quarterly* 55 (1991): 161–179.

Sirken, M. G. "Error Effects of Survey Questionnaires on the Public's Assessments of Health Risks." *American Journal of Public Health* 76 (1986): 367–368.

Skogan, W. G. "Victimization Surveys and Criminal Justice Planning." *University of Cincinnati Law Review* 45 (1976): 167–206.

Slovic, P. "Perception of Risk." *Science* 236 (Apr. 17, 1987): 280–285.

———, B. Fischhoff, and S. Lichtenstein. "Rating the Risks." *Environment* 21 (1979): 14–20, 36–39.

Smith, R. C. "The Magazines' Smoking Habit." *Columbia Journalism Review* 16 (1978): 29–31.

Smith, T. W. "Poll Report: The Sexual Revolution?" *Public Opinion Quarterly* 54 (1990): 415–435.

Stallings, R. A. "Media Discourse and the Social Construction of Risk." *Social Problems* 37 (1990): 180–193.

Stein, M. L. "The Multicultural Approach." *Editor and Publisher,* pp. 12–13, Sept. 1, 1990.

Tankard, J. W., Jr., and M. Ryan. "News Source Perceptions of Accuracy of Science Coverage." *Journalism Quarterly* 51 (1974): 218–225, 234.

Tennen, H., and G. Affleck. "Blaming Others for Threatening Events." *Psychological Bulletin* 108 (1990): 209–232.

Tichenor, P. J., C. N. Olien, A. Harrison, and G. Donohue. "Mass Communication Systems and Communication Accuracy in Science News Reporting." *Journalism Quarterly* 47 (1970): 673–683.

Times-Mirror Company. "The People and the Press," part I, Jan. 1986.

———. "The People and the Press," part II, Sept. 1986.

Tuchman, G. *Making News.* New York: Free Press, 1978.

Turk, J. V. "Public Relations' Influence on the News." *Newspaper Research Journal* 7(4) (1986): 15–27.

Turk, J. V., et al. "Hispanic-Americans in the News in Two Southwestern Cities." *Journalism Quarterly* 66 (1989): 107–113.

Turner, R. H. "The Mass Media and Preparation for Natural Disaster." In *Disasters and the Mass Media,* Proceedings of the Committee on Disasters and the Mass Media Workshop, pp. 281–292. Washington, DC: National Academy of Sciences, 1980.

———, J. Nigg, and D. H. Paz. *Waiting for Disaster: Earthquake Watching in Southern California.* Berkeley, CA: University of California Press, 1986.

Tversky, A., and D. Kahneman. "Availability: A Heuristic for Judging Frequency and Probability." *Cognitive Psychology* 4 (1973): 207–232.

———. "The Framing of Decisions and the Psychology of Choice." *Science* 211 (1981): 453–458.

———. "Judgment under Uncertainty: Heuristics and Biases." *Science* 185 (1974): 1124–1131.

Warner, K., et al. "Cigarette Advertising and Magazine Coverage of Hazards of Smoking." *New England Journal of Medicine* 326 (Jan. 30, 1992): 305–309.

Warr, M. "The Accuracy of Public Beliefs about Crime." *Social Forces* 59 (1980): 456–470.

Watts, M. *Silent Violence: Food, Famine and Peasantry in Northern Nigeria.* Berkeley, CA: University of California Press, 1983.

Weaver, D. H. "Media Agenda-Setting and Media." In D. C. Whitney, E. Wartella, and S. Windahl, eds. *Mass Communication Review Yearbook 3*, pp. 537–554. Beverly Hills, CA: Sage, 1982.

Weiner, S. L. "Tampons and Toxic Shock Syndrome: Consumer Protection or Public Confusion?" In H. M. Sapolsky, ed. *Consuming Fears.* New York: Basic Books, 1986.

Weir, D. *The Bhopal Syndrome.* San Francisco: Sierra Book Club, 1987.

Weis, W. L., and C. Burke. "Media Control of Tobacco Advertising: An Unhealthy Addiction." *Journal of Communication* 36(4) (1986): 59–69.

Weiss, C. H., and E. Singer, with P. Endreny. *The Reporting of Social Science in the National Media.* New York: Russell Sage, 1988.

Whitney, D. C. "The Media and the People: Americans' Experience with the News Media—A Fifty-Year Review." New York: Columbia University, Gannett Center Working Paper, 1986.

Wiegman, G., et al. "Newspaper Coverage of Hazards and the Reactions of Readers." *Journalism Quarterly* 66 (1989): 846–852, 863.

Wilkins, L., and P. Patterson. "Risk Analysis and the Construction of News." *Journal of Communication* 37(3) (1987): 80–92. The quote is from B. Fischhoff, "Judgmental Aspects of Risk Analysis." Unpublished manuscript, Decision Research, Inc., Eugene, OR, 1984.

Wilson, R., and E. A. Crouch. "Risk Assessment and Comparisons: An Introduction." *Science* 236 (Apr. 17, 1987): 267–270.

Winsten, J., and W. DeJong. "The Use of Mass Media in Substance Abuse Prevention." *Health Affairs* 9(2) (1990): 30–46.

Winter, J. P. "Contingent Conditions in the Agenda-Setting Process." In G. C. Wilhoit and H. de Bock, eds. *Mass Communication Review Yearbook 2*, pp. 235–244. Beverly Hills, CA: Sage, 1981.

Zimmerman, C., and R. A. Bauer. "The Effect of an Audience on What Is Remembered." In E. E. Maccoby, T. M. Newcomb, and E. L. Hartley, eds. *Readings in Social Psychology*, 3d ed., pp. 65–71. New York: Holt, Rinehart and Winston, 1958.

Zucker, H. G. "The Variable Nature of News Media Influence." In B. D. Ruben, ed. *Communication Yearbook 2.* New Brunswick, NJ: Transaction Books, 1978.

Appendix A
Categories of Hazard and Selection Rules

CATEGORIES OF HAZARD

The system of categories we adopted is built on the Hohenemser *et al.* (1983) classification of technological hazards but designed to accommodate other classes of hazards that appear in the media as well. Specifically, the system consists of the following categories, which are *not* mutually exclusive:

1. Natural disasters
2. Activities with benefits and costs (risks)
3. Energy hazards
4. Materials hazards
5. Complex technologies
6. Chronic and acute illnesses

The first category is largely self-explanatory; it includes hazards such as drought, storms, earthquakes. We have added poverty to this group, knowing it is not a "natural" hazard in the sense of the others, but because of our special interest in media coverage of poverty as a hazardous condition associated with an array of health risks. We also recognize that some "natural" disasters may result from unnatural (i.e., man-made) interventions.

The second category consists of activities—such as swimming, skiing, jogging—that are pleasurable but may lead unintentionally to injury or death. In some cases, these are covered as "energy hazards" in the Hohen-emser classification, and wherever this occurs we will note the two versions. The activity format is designed for those cases where the media cover a hazard—e.g., swimming—and the focus is on the activity, not the technology that may be involved (e.g., not on "home pools" but on dangerous undertows). "Accidents" is the lay term that covers many of our activities and many of Hohenemser's energy hazards as well.

Categories 3 and 4 are those of Hohenemser and his colleagues, but with other technologies and their hazards added as necessary. Category 5 includes complex technologies such as organ transplants, heart surgery, gene therapy, abortion, medical care (inadequacies), health care (inadequacies), and euthanasia.

The category of illness does not appear at all in the Hohenemser scheme. In general, when a media story focuses on a particular cause or contributory factor in an illness—e.g., asbestos or smoking in cancer—we will code the story under that "risk factor," not under the illness. On the other hand, if the story focuses on the illness per se (i.e., on cancer, which may develop as a result of many causes), or on prevalence or treatment or consequences of the illness, we will code the story under the illness.

1. Natural Disaster

101	Avalanche
122	Deforestation
102	Drought
104	Earthquake
118	Famine
106	Flood (storm-caused flood is coded as storm)
107	Frost/Freeze
112	Lightning
119	Overpopulation
120	Poverty
110	Storms (wind) (e.g., hurricane, typhoon, snow, tornado)
116	Volcano
121	Natural Disaster—general

2. Activities (Benefit/Cost)

201	Ballooning
202	Biking (bicycles)—injuries
203	Boating (recreational boating—drowning)
204	Bullfight—accidents
205	Camping—accidents
206	Contact Sports—football, hockey, boxing, soccer, wrestling

207 Diving
208 Exercise (in general)—heat exhaustion, injuries, heart attack
209 Fasting
210 Fishing—drowning, other accidents
211 Gymnastics and dancing—injuries (trampolines, falls)
212 Horse Riding—falls, including racing
222 Ice—drowning
224 Hunting
213 Mountain Climbing—falls (see also Falls, in Energy Hazard)
214 Mushroom Picking—poison
215 Occupational hazard (except those specified in Energy/Materials lists, or home work)
216 Racing Car (motor-vehicle racing)—crash
217 Skiing—injuries (downhill skiing, injuries)
218 Skydiving—accidents
219 Spectator Sport
220 Swimming—drowning, exposure
221 Tennis—accidents
223 Water-skiing

3. Energy Hazards

301 Amusement Rides—accidents
302 Appliances—fire
303 Appliances—shock
304 Appliances—other malfunctions
305 Auto—crashes
306 Auto and other motor-vehicle—defects
307 Aviation—commercial—crashes
308 Aviation—military—crashes
309 Aviation—private—crashes
374 Aviation (aircraft)—defects
310 Bridges—collapse
311 Building—collapse
312 Bus—crashes
313 Chain Saws—accidents
314 Coal Gasification—accidents
315 Coal Mining—accidents
316 Construction—falls and other accidents (except cranes)
317 Conveyor Belt—accidents
318 Cranes—accidents
319 Dams—failure
320 Dynamite Blasts—accidents
321 Electrical Power (distribution)—explosions
322 Electrical Power Generation—accidents, power failure
323 Elevators—falls

324 Explosions (not otherwise specified)
370 Falls (unclassified)
325 Fires (other than skyscrapers and forest)—burns/smoke inhalation
326 Fire—toxic smoke
327 Fireworks—accidents
328 Forest/grass fires
329 Gas Drilling—accidents
373 Gasoline Leaks, vapors
371 Gas (unspecified) Explosion
372 Gas (unspecified) Leak
369 Gold Mining—accidents
330 Handguns (and other firearms)—shootings
331 Helicopter—crashes
332 High Voltage Wires—electric fields
333 Irradiation
334 LNG—explosions
335 Medical X-rays—radiation
336 Methane—explosion
337 Microwave Ovens—radiation
338 Motorcycles—accidents
339 Motor Vehicle/Pedestrian Collisions
340 Munitions Depot—explosions
341 Natural Gas—explosions
342 Noise
343 Nuclear War—blast
344 Nursery Equipment and Toys—unsafe
345 Office Equipment—accidents
346 Oil Drilling—accidents
347 Oil Refinery—accidents
348 Pothole
349 Power Motors—accidents
350 Propane—explosions
351 Radiation (other than specifically nuclear or medical)
352 Roads—collapse
353 Shipping—commercial, ferry, military—accidents
354 Skateboards—falls
355 Skyscrapers—fire
356 Smoking—fires
357 Snowmobiles—collisions
358 Space Heaters
359 Space Vehicles—crashes (risk to people on ground)
360 Space Vehicles, Shuttle—(risk to passengers)
375 Steam Heat
361 Submarine—accidents
362 Subways—fire, derailment, crashes

363 Sunlight (too much, too little)
364 Toys—see Nursery Equipment
365 Tractors—accidents
366 Trains—crashes
367 Trucks—accidents
368 Accidents, General (not otherwise specified)

4. Materials Hazards

401 Acid Rain
     Agent Orange—code under Dioxin
     Air Pollution, see Chemicals, toxic effects
402 Alcohol—accidents
403 Alcohol—chronic effects
404 Ammonia Gas—toxic
405 Antibiotics—bacterial resistance
406 Asbestos Insulation—toxic effects
407 Asbestos Spray—toxic effects
408 Aspartame—toxic effects
409 Aspirin—overdose
410 Auto—CO pollution
411 Auto—lead pollution
412 Auto (and boat)—pollution, other than CO or lead
413 Benzene
414 Cadmium—toxic effects
415 Caffeine—chronic effects
416 Chemicals (other or unspecified)—toxic effects, including air or
     water pollution (and herbicides)
417 Chemicals—spills
418 Cholesterol
419 Coal Burning—NO_3 pollution
420 Coal Burning—SO_2 pollution
421 Coal Burning—other pollution
422 Coal Mining—black lung
423 Contraceptive IUDs—side effects
424 Contraceptive Pills—side effects
425 Contraceptive, Other—side effects
426 Darvon—overdose
427 DDT—toxic effects
428 Deforestation—CO_2 release
429 DES—animal feed—human toxicity
430 DES—human toxicity
431 Dioxin—toxic effects
432 Drugs—addiction—toxic effects
433 Drugs—side effects, and mistaken uses
434 Dyes—toxicity

435 EDB (ethyldibromide)
436 Electronics Mfg.—toxic effects
437 Estrogens—human toxicity
438 Fertilizer—NO_3 pollution
439 Fluorocarbons—ozone depletion
440 Formaldehyde
441 Fossil Fuels—CO_2 release
    Garbage Disposal—see Chemicals—air pollution
442 Hair Dyes—coal-tar exposure
443 Hexachlorophene—toxic effects
444 Home Pools—drowning
445 Laetrile—toxic effects
446 Lead Paint—human toxicity
447 Lye
448 Meat—contaminated (*not* focused on Food Poisoning, which see)
449 Mercury—toxic effects
450 Methyl Isocyanate
451 Minoxidil
452 Mirex Pesticide—toxic effects
453 Nerve Gas—accidents
454 Nerve Gas—war use
455 Nitrite Preservative—toxic effects
456 Nuclear Fuel—radiation release
457 Nuclear Reactor and Nuclear Weapons Plant—radiation release
458 Nuclear Tests—fallout
459 Nuclear War—radiation effects
460 Nuclear Waste—radiation effects
461 Oil Tankers (pipelines)—spills
462 PCBs—toxic effects
463 Packaging
464 Pesticides (other than specified)—human toxicity
465 Poisonous Plants
466 Product Tampering
467 PVC—human toxicity
468 Radon—toxic effects
469 Recombinant DNA—harmful release
470 Rubber Manufacture—toxic exposure
471 Saccharin—cancer
472 Silicone Implants—toxic effects
473 Smoking (including chewing and snuff)—chronic effects
474 SST—ozone depletion
475 Sulfite Preservative—toxicity
476 Tampons—toxic shock
477 Taconite Mining—water pollution
478 Thalidomide—side effects
479 Toothpicks—injuries

480   Toxic Waste (including air and water pollution) (unspecified)—toxic effects
481   Trichloroethylene—toxic effects
482   Two, 4, 5-T Herbicide—toxic effects
483   Underwater Construction—accidents
484   Uranium Mining and Processing—radiation
485   Vaccines—defective
486   Vaccines—side effects
487   Valium—misuse
488   VDTs
489   Warfarin—human toxicity
490   Water Chlorination—toxic effects
491   Water Fluoridation—toxic effects
492   Water Pollution—see Chemicals, toxic effects
493   Wood Preservatives—toxic effects
494   Zeranol (cattle feed)—toxic effects
495   Hazards (general or multiple or unknown)

5. Complex Technologies (subcategory of Materials Hazards)

501   Abortion
502   Bottle Feeding
503   Chorionic Villus Sampling (C.V.S.)
504   Diagnostic Procedures
505   Euthanasia
506   Gene Splicing (see Recombinant DNA, but treat as complex technology)
507   Gene Therapy
508   Health Care—inadequacies
509   Heart Surgery
510   Medical Care—inadequacies (including fraud)
511   Medical Care—withholding, for religious reasons
512   Medical Devices—defects
513   Organ Transplants (including artificial organs)
514   Surgery—other than heart or transplant
515   Transfusion Medicine

6. Illnesses: Chronic

601   Aging—diseases of
602   AIDS
603   A.L.S.
604   Alzheimer's Disease
605   Anxiety Attacks

678 Artery Disease
682 Arthritis
681 Asthma
606 Birth Defects—in general (other than specified below)—including mental retardation, Down's Syndrome
684 Blindness
607 Brown Lung Disease
686 Brucellosis
608 Cancer
609 Chlamydia
610 Deafness
611 Diabetes
612 Emphysema
613 Epidermolysis Bullosa
614 Genes—defects predisposing to illness
615 Glaucoma
616 Gonorrhea
617 Genital Herpes
618 Heart Disease
619 Hemophilia
620 Hypertension
621 Kidney Disease
622 Marfan Syndrome
623 Mineral Deficiency, vitamin deficiency
677 Menière's disease
624 Mental Illness (including retardation)
626 Multiple Sclerosis
627 Neurologic Malfunction (e.g., heart stopping)
628 Obesity
629 Osteoporosis
679 Parkinson's Disease
630 Polio (1960)
632 Sickle-Cell Anemia
633 Sleep Disorders
634 Spina Bifida
635 Tuberculosis
     (Vitamin Deficiency—see Mineral Deficiency)
636 Disability (in general—physical and mental)

Illnesses: Acute

651 Aneurism
652 Childbirth (including Caesarean)
653 Choking
654 Cholera

680 Cystic Fibrosis
655 Diarrheal Dehydration
656 Encephalitis
657 Endometriosis
658 Exposure
659 Food Poisoning (if deliberate, see Product tampering)
661 Heat Stroke
662 Hepatitis
663 Influenza
664 Insect Stings—allergy, infections
665 Legionnaire's Disease
666 Measles
667 Plague
       Polio—see Chronic
668 Premature Birth
669 Pregnancy
685 Reye's Syndrome
683 Rocky Mountain Spotted Fever
670 Rubella
671 Smallpox (1960)
672 Stroke
673 Sudden (unknown) Death
674 Tattoo/allergy
675 Viruses—serious diseases (several, or in general)
676 Whooping Cough

SELECTION RULES
In General:

Select all stories which either (a) focus on the hazard specified in our "Categories of Hazard" list or (b) give substantial and/or prominent reference to the hazard, even if it is not the focus. To meet the "substantial and/or prominent" condition, the hazard must be discussed in one-third of the article (substantial) or in one of the first two paragraphs (prominent).

Below are more detailed guidelines for the six categories of hazard:

1. Natural disasters

2. Activities with benefits and costs (risks)

3. Energy hazards

4. Materials hazards

5. Complex technologies

6. Chronic and acute illnesses

1. Select any story *focused* on a *natural hazard capable* of causing disability/ death even if no deaths are mentioned (e.g., drought; major storms like hurricanes, tornadoes; earthquakes; floods).

a. A story on *famine* is automatically included.

b. A story on *poverty* is included only (1) if there is an explicit mention of risk of dying/disability, *except* (2) during "inclusive"[1] period, when all stories about poverty would be selected.

2. Stories focused on *activities with potential good/bad consequences* are selected *only* (1) if there is a substantial/prominent explicit mention of risk, *or* (2) during "inclusive" period (e.g., stories about swimming, biking, skiing, jogging).

3, 4, and 5. Select all *focused on* technological hazards (Energy and Material) on Hohenemser's list, plus others added for this study (e.g., organ transplants, heart surgery, gene therapy, abortion), even if there is no mention of risk; if in doubt, the presumption is in favor of its ability to cause disability/ death.

But *exclude* (a) stories focused on *legislation* dealing with the hazard, unless there is a substantial/prominent mention of risk; (b) stories dealing with money costs of cleaning up hazard, unless there is a substantial/prominent mention of risk; (c) stories about legal or administrative aspects, unless there is a substantial/prominent mention of risk. In other words, stories that simply name the "toxic waste" hazard without specifying/focusing on the risks, are excluded; similarly, stories which simply name the hazard of "drunk driving" without specifying/focusing on the risks are excluded.

We will select stories about drug addiction as a physiological risk. However, we will not take stories that are concerned exclusively with the drug trade, and/or law enforcement efforts to combat it.

Other examples:

Include "biocidal" risks—e.g., acid rain.

We would *take* a story about subway fires, but *not* a story about the general deterioration of subway service.

Nuclear war/weapons (energy hazard):

Include stories focused on *issues* **of disarmament** or defense, whether or not there is a mention of risk.

Exclude (a) political propaganda **stories; (b)** stories about demonstrations unless there is a substantial/prominent **mention** of risk issues. *All* arms talk stories are to be taken as "Inclusive" stories (thus selected only during the November/December intensive reading period).

Nuclear weapons related stories:

a. If the story is primarily about the technology/capability of the weapon as hardware, we will *omit* it.

b. If the story is about the technology and its relation to deterrence, we will *take* it.

---

[1]See pp. 193–194, below.

c. If the story is about flaws and vulnerability in individual and/or general weapons systems, we will *take* it.

6. Select all stories *focused on* chronic or acute illnesses that cause death or disability, whether or not risk is mentioned, and those focused on *causes* of such illnesses.

But *exclude* (a) stories focused on *costs* of treatment—e.g., dialysis costs; (b) stories on treatment, unless there is substantial mention of risk; (c) stories about hospital strikes, unless there is substantial mention of risk—*except* for inclusive selection. *Always exclude* stories focused, narrowly, on personnel involved—e.g., a story about DeVries.

Additional Selection Rules

—*Include* book reviews.

—*Include* stories that report accidents or illnesses of notable individuals. Follow-up stories that focus on successive stages of accident or illness are taken. Follow-up stories that focus on the notable personality, family, and so forth, will *not* be taken.

—*Exclude* stories involving "unique" risks—e.g., attempt on Pope's life.

—*Exclude* print obituaries (unless as major news story, with emphasis on cause of death) and letters. However, take television obits.

—*Exclude* stories focused on capital punishment as an issue.

—*Exclude* war, except nuclear war.

—*Exclude* stories focused on public interest organizations even when their primary interest is fighting specific risks.

—*Exclude* sex abuse stories, other than at day-care centers.

—*Exclude* stories about risks to embryos, per se.

Pieces composed of several small items, each with its own small headline, will be selected on an item-by-item basis.

For legal aftermaths of hazards (e.g., Dalkon Shield)—select if a substantial/prominent mention of the risk is made (except in inclusive reading period, when we would take all).

Beginning November 4 and running through December 30, we are also selecting "inclusively," to pick up stories which do *not* focus on risk, but which concern topics that could invite a more substantial discussion of risk (e.g., stories on the space shuttle that barely mention risk, or stories that focus on legal, fiscal,or administrative rather than risk-aspects of toxic waste or nuclear energy problems).

Because our inclusive reading is an attempt to get at the *absence* of the attention to risk, it is hard to be very specific about guidelines. Three rules, do, however, set some boundaries:

a. Stories about *kinds* of hazards that we would not take under regular reading—for example, common cold, sprained finger, sex abuse, and so forth—are not taken for the inclusive reading. Inclusive reading is intended to pick up various journalistic treatments of the specified hazard categories, NOT to pick up new hazard categories.

b. Opinion pieces, editorials, book/theater/TV reviews and sports are *not* read for inclusive material (i.e., they either have to qualify as regular stories or not at all). For newspapers, this means that primarily the main news sections are being read for inclusive selection.

c. There have to be some specific grounds for deeming an article as having a potential for more discussion of risk (e.g., a *WSJ* story about the financial difficulties of LILCO may not, but could conceivably, have a substantial reference to the safety concerns about the Shoreham nuclear plant). Similarly, we aren't taking inclusively every story that mentions an auto (e.g., new car sales) or airplane (e.g., new fare wars) just because those vehicles can represent energy hazards.

There may be a story that, in itself, doesn't give the reader any reason to think about hazard or risk; however, another version of the same story may chance to raise a health/safety concern. Having been thus alerted by the one account, we would inclusively select all stories on that subject, however absent even the implications of risk might be from the other versions.

NB: Ads for therapies (e.g., stop smoking) and to locate victims (e.g., DES, asbestos) are also part of the media contribution to risk awareness. We, however, are not selecting them.

Selection Checks

Check stories against these criteria:

1. Is the story about a hazard (i.e., a potential threat to life)?
   (If not, don't select.)

2. Does it mention a specific risk (of death or injury, not necessarily quantified) associated with the hazard?

3. Does it *quantify* the risk?

Appendix B
Examples of Coding Forms*

*Appendix B includes a copy of the General Coding Form, on which all news stories were coded, and a copy of the Materials Hazards Coding Form, which was specific to that hazard category. Although most coding items were identical across hazard categories, some items were specific to each hazard. Copies of the other hazard coding forms are available from the authors on request.

CODE FORM: RISK STORIES

CASE ID _____

1. Headline, including subhead (If subject is not apparent from headline, <u>add</u> description of what story is about—e.g., seat belt regulations)

_____

_____

_____

2. Type of item in which reference to hazard occurs:
   1 News/feature story
   2 Editorial
   3 Column (i.e., opinion piece)
   4 Department, Q & A
   5 Book review
   6 TV nonfiction feature
   7 Other media item (specify)

3. What types of hazard are mentioned in the item (or <u>might</u> have been mentioned, if this is an inclusive story)? CODE AS MANY AS APPLY.

   1 Natural disaster (specify name and code) _____

   _____

   2 Activities with benefits and costs (specify name and code)

   _____

   3 Energy hazard (specify name and code) _____

   _____

   4 Materials hazard (specify name and code) _____

   _____

   5 Chronic or acute illness (specify name and code) _____

   _____

   6 Complex technology (specify name and code) _____

   _____

   7 Emergent risks (specify name and code) _____

   _____

   9 Miscellaneous, other (specify name and code) _____

   _____

4. If more than one hazard has been circled in (Q. 3), above, which is the most important hazard? Which does the story focus on? Code one of numbers 1–9.

5. Does the story refer to this as a "new" hazard?
   1 Yes
   2 No (answer A)

   A. Is this a new hazard? (To be coded by ES or PE)
      1 Yes
      2 No

6. If more than one hazard has been circled in (Q. 3), above, does the hazard which is the focus of the story result from or lead to another hazard mentioned in the story? (E.g., a truck accident which results in an oil spill; an explosion which results in a fire, etc.)
   1 Yes, one hazard results from or leads to another hazard mentioned in the story
   2 No, there is no "causal chain"; the hazards are separate and distinct

7. Is a hazard the focus of the item, or is there only an ancillary mention of a hazard, or is there no mention at all?
   1 Focus (answer A)
      A. Is hazard mentioned in headline or first two paragraphs ("prominent"), is it the subject of ⅓ the story or more ("substantial"), or is it both prominent and substantial?
         1 Prominent only
         2 Substantial only
         3 Both
   2 Ancillary (neither prominent nor substantial, but some mention) } for inclusive stories only
   3 No mention at all (Skip to Q. 10).

8. Fraction of item devoted to discussion of hazard(s):
   1 Parenthetical phrase only
   2 One or two sentences
   3 More than a sentence or two, but no more than a third
   4 More than a third, but less than two thirds
   5 More than two thirds

9. Where does the mention of hazard first appear?
   1 In headline
   2 In first paragraph
   3 Not in first paragraph, but in first third of item
   4 Not in first third of item

10. Media
    01 Times
    02 News
    03 Wall Street Journal
    04 Amsterdam News
    05 Newsweek
    06 Time
    07 CBS News
    08 NBC News
    09 ABC News
    10 Channel 5
    11 Ladies Home Journal
    12 Ebony
    13 Essence
    14 New York Magazine
    15 Prevention
    16 Other (specify) (for TV features)

11. Date (month/day/year)

12. Day (Circle one): 1 M 2 T 3 W 4 TH 5 FR 6 SA 7 SU 9 DNA (MAG ONLY)

13. Section and first page for print media <u>or</u> time of newscast:

Daily papers (section letter or number and page) _____

Sunday papers (section letter or number and page) _____

Newsmagazines (page) _____

Newscast (time of story in newscast or page #) _____

TV feature (time) _____

14. Special placement/treatment
    A. Newspapers
        1 Front page
        2 First page of section other than first section
        3 Sunday magazine or book review cover story
        9 No special placement
    B. Magazines
        1 Cover story
        9 No special placement
    C. Television news
        1 Interview or film
        2 No special treatment; anchor only
        8 D.K.
    D. Television Feature
        1 Always prime time

Codeform   3

15. Amount of space/time devoted to item

    Column inches (to nearest inch) _____

                                    OR

    No. of lines _____

    No. of minutes (if feature or WNEW) _____

16. Visuals (Print and nonfiction feature only)

        1 Yes (Code A–F)   2 No (Skip to Q. 17)

        A. Photo
           1 Yes
           2 No

        B. Graph, Chart
           1 Yes
           2 No

        C. Cartoon
           1 Yes
           2 No

        D. Drawing (except cartoon, graph)
           1 Yes
           2 No

        E. Map
           1 Yes
           2 No

        F. Other (specify)
           1 Yes
           2 No

17. Source of story

    A. For newspapers
           1 By-lined writer/reporter, columnist (specify)

           _____

           2 AP (if named writer, specify) _____

           3 UPI (if named writer, specify) _____

           8 Other (other newspaper service, "special to the. . . ." other
             newspaper or periodical) (specify) _____

           _____

           9 No specified source

B. For magazines
    1 Bylined staff writer/reporter (specify first-named only)

_____

    9 No byline

C. For television newscast

    1 Anchor only (specify) _____

    2 Special reporter as well (specify) _____
    8 D.K.

18. Is the story designated as part of a series?
    1 Yes
    2 No

19. As far as you know, is this part of a continuing story?
    1 Yes
    2 No
    3 D.K.

20. Does this story:
    1 Report <u>only</u> a self-contained occurrence of a hazard (e.g., a fire, someone's illness, a car crash, a release of toxic gas) with <u>no mention</u> of risk factors <u>or</u> issues? (ANSWER Q. 21–26)
    2 Report an event or condition <u>potentially treated</u> as risky, but with <u>no specific mention</u> of risk(s) (e.g., mountain climbing) or an event or condition <u>potentially risky</u>, but not a risk in this case (e.g., a power failure that might have caused death or injury but did not in this case, a near-miss of an airplane crash)? (ANSWER Q. 21–26)
    3 Report on issues and/or data related to a hazard or to a hazardous event/condition? (SKIP TO APPROPRIATE HAZARD SECTION)

21. Does the story have a geographic focus? That is, does it talk about a hazard in a specific place (e.g., a train crash on Long Island)?
    1 Yes (answer A, B)
    2 No

A. What is the geographic location? (USE PRECODES) _____

B. Does the story indicate that the hazard is more general or widespread than the geographic focus suggests?
    1 Yes (answer B1)
    2 No

B1. What other hazard location is referred to? (Code highest code that applies)
  1 One or more additional localities or states
  2 Nation at large
  3 One or more additional countries
  4 World in general

22. Does the story mention property damage in connection with the hazard?
  1 Yes (answer A, B)
  2 No

  A. Amount of property damage
    1 Less than $10,000
    2 $10,000–$100,000
    3 $100,000–$1 million
    4 $1 million–$10 million
    5 $10 million–$100 million
    6 $100 million–$1 billion
    7 More than $1 billion
    8 No dollar amount given (answer A1)

  A1. Amount of damage
    1 "Small" (1–10 homes/cars)
    2 "Medium" (10–100 homes/cars)
    3 "Large" (100–1,000 homes/cars)
    4 Massive (more than 1,000 homes/cars)

  B. Is property damage actual or potential?
    1 Actual
    2 Potential
    3 Both (use this code only if the amount specified in A, above, includes both actual and potential damage)
    4 Both, but numbers coded above refer to actual damage only

23. Does story mention injuries or illnesses resulting from hazard?
  1 Yes (answer A, B)
  2 No

  A. How many cases of injury/illness were mentioned?
    1 Less than 10
    2 10–100
    3 100–1,000
    4 1,000–10,000
    5 10,000–100,000
    6 10^5–
    7 10^6–
    8 10^7–
    9 No specific number mentioned (answer A1)

Codeform   6

A1.   No. of injuries/illnesses
  1   A few (Less than 10)
  2   Some (10–20)
  3   Many (20–50)
  4   Scores (50–100)
  5   Hundreds (100–1,000)
  6   More than hundreds (More than 1,000)

B.   Are injuries/illnesses actual or potential?
  1   Actual
  2   Potential
  3   Both (use this code only if both are included in number coded in A, above)
  4   Both, but numbers coded above refer to actual injuries only

24.   Does story mention deaths in connection with hazard?
  1   Yes (answer A, B)
  2   No

A.   How many deaths were mentioned?
  1   Less than 10
  2   10–100
  3   100–1000
  4   1000–10,000
  5   10,000–100,000
  6   10^5 –
  7   10^6 –
  8   10^7 –
  9   No specific number mentioned (answer A1)

A1.   No. of deaths
  1   A few (Less than 10)
  2   Some (10–20)
  3   Many (20–50)
  4   Scores (50–100)
  5   Hundreds (100–1000)
  6   More than hundreds (More than 1000)

B.   Are deaths actual or potential?
  1   Actual
  2   Potential
  3   Both (use this code only if both are included in number coded in A, above)
  4   Both, but numbers coded above refer to actual deaths only

25. Does the story mention benefits (or pleasures) associated with the hazard?
    1 Yes
    2 No

26. Is the event a "legal" event (e.g., a trial or a lawsuit?)
    1 Yes
    2 No

NOW SKIP TO Q. 100

MATERIALS HAZARDS

1. Hazard name (and 4-digit code) _____

2. Does the item (CODE AS MANY AS APPLY)
   2-1 Discuss an event involving a materials hazard (e.g., a chemical spill)
   2-2 Cite data pertaining to a materials hazard (e.g., the number of people who die as a result of asbestos exposure each year)
   2-3 Discuss causes or contributory factors of materials hazard
   2-4 Discuss prevention of hazard
   2-5 Discuss ethical issues
   2-6 Discuss litigation related to hazard

   2-8 Other (specify) _____

   A. (If more than one) Which of these is the most important, in terms of emphasis? Select one of codes 1-8 above.

3. Does the story have a geographic focus? That is, does it talk about a materials hazard in a specific place (e.g., an oil spill on Long Island)?
   1 Yes (answer A, B)
   2 No

   A. What is the geographic location? (USE PRECODES) _____

   B. Does this story indicate that the hazard is more general or widespread than the geographic focus suggests?
      1 Yes (answer B1)
      2 No

   B1. What other hazard location is referred to? (Code highest code which applies)
      1 One or more additional localities or states
      2 Nation at large
      3 One or more additional countries
      4 World in general

4. Does the story mention property damage in connection with the materials hazard?
   1 Yes (answer A, B)
   2 No

   A. Amount of property damage
      1 Less than $10,000
      2 $10,000-$100,000
      3 $100,000-$1 million
      4 $1 million-$10 million
      5 $10 million-$100 million
      6 $100 million-$1 billion
      7 More than $1 billion
      8 No dollar amount given (answer A1)

Codeform   1

A1. Amount of damage
   1 "Small" (1–10 homes/cars)
   2 "Medium" (10–100 homes/cars)
   3 "Large" (100–1,000 homes/cars)
   4 Massive (more than 1,000 homes/cars)

B. Is property damage actual or potential?
   1 Actual
   2 Potential
   3 Both (use this code only if the amount specified in A, above, includes both actual and potential damage)
   4 Both, but numbers coded above refer to actual damage only

5. Does story mention injuries or illnesses resulting from materials hazard?
   1 Yes (answer A, B, C)
   2 No

A. What are the illnesses or conditions? (Give names and 4-digit codes; 9999 = no code)

   _____   _____

   _____   _____

B. How many cases of injury/illness were mentioned?
   1 Less than 10
   2 10–100
   3 100–1,000
   4 1,000–10,000
   5 10,000–100,000
   6 10^5–
   7 10^6–
   8 10^7–
   9 No specific number mentioned (answer B1)

B1. No. of injuries/illnesses
   1 A few (Less than 10)
   2 Some (10–20)
   3 Many (20–50)
   4 Scores (50–100)
   5 Hundreds (100–1,000)
   6 More than hundreds (More than 1,000)

C. Are injuries/illnesses actual or potential?
   1 Actual
   2 Potential
   3 Both (Use this code only if both are included in number coded in A, above)
   4 Both, but numbers coded above refer to actual injuries only

6. Does story mention deaths in connection with materials hazard?
    1 Yes (answer A, B)
    2 No

  A. How many deaths were mentioned?
      1 Less than 10
      2 10–100
      3 100–1,000
      4 1,000–10,000
      5 10,000–100,000
      6 10^5–
      7 10^6–
      8 10^7–
      9 No specific number mentioned (answer A1)

  A1. No. of deaths
      1 A few (Less than 10)
      2 Some (10–20)
      3 Many (20–50)
      4 Scores (50–100)
      5 Hundreds (100–1,000)
      6 More than hundreds (More than 1,000)

  B. Are deaths actual or potential?
      1 Actual
      2 Potential
      3 Both (Use this code only if both are included in number coded in A, above)
      4 Both, but numbers coded above refer to actual deaths only

7. Does story mention the annual mortality (i.e., the number of deaths due to the materials hazard in question)?
    1 Yes (answer A, B)
    2 No

  A. What is the annual mortality for the hazard?
      1 1–10 people
      2 10–100
      3 100–1,000
      4 1,000–10,000
      5 10,000–100,000
      6 100,000–1,000,000
      7 10^6–10^7
      8 10^7–10^8
      9 More than 10^8
      0 No specific number mentioned (answer A1)

A1. No. of deaths per year
    1 A few (Less than 10)
    2 Some (10–20)
    3 Many (20–50)
    4 Scores (50–100)
    5 Hundreds (100–1,000)
    6 More than hundreds (More than 1,000)

B. For what unit is the annual mortality reported?
    1 U.S.

    2 One state (which?) _____

    3 One city (which?) _____

    4 One country other than U.S. (which?) _____

    5 World

    6 Other (specify) _____

    7 None; no unit specified

8. Does the story explicitly mention:

A. The size of the population at risk?
    1 Yes (answer A1)
    2 No

A1.
    1 1–10
    2 10–100
    3 100–1,000
    4 1,000–10,000
    5 10,000–100,000
    6 100,000–1 million
    7 1 million–10 million
    8 10 million–100 million
    9 More than 100 million
    0 Qualitative estimates only (specify)

_____

B. The spatial extent of the hazard?
    1 Yes (answer B1)
    2 No

B1.
    1 Square meter
    2 1–100 square meters (e.g., up to size of a small house)
    3 100–10,000 square meters (a city block)
    4 Neighborhood
    5 Small region (part of a city)

6 Region (county)
7 Subcontinental (state, country)
8 Continental
9 Global
0 Qualitative estimates only (specify)

C. The actual or expected persistence of the hazard?
1 Yes (answer C1)
2 No

C1.

1 Less than 1 minute
2 1–10 minutes
3 10–100 minutes
4 2 hours–17 hours
5 17 hours–1 week
6 1 week–2½ months
7 2½ months–2 years
8 1 year–20 years
9 More than 20 years
0 Qualitative estimates only (specify)

D. Amount of delay in the onset of consequences?
1 Yes (answer D1)
2 No

D1.

1 Less than 1 minute
2 1–10 minutes
3 10–100 minutes
4 2 hours–17 hours
5 17 hours–1 week
6 1 week–2½ months
7 2½ months–2 years
8 1 year–20 years
9 More than 20 years
0 Qualitative estimates only (specify)

E. Whether or not transgenerational effects occur?
1 Yes (answer E1)
2 No

E1.

3 No transgenerational effects
6 Potential effect on one subsequent generation (including fetuses)
9 Potential effects on more than one subsequent generation

9. What proportion of the story is devoted to risks (property damage, illness, injury, or death)?
   1 Less than ¼
   2 ¼–½
   3 ½–¾
   4 More than ¾

10. Does the story mention benefits (or pleasures) associated with the hazard?
    1 Yes (answer A, B, C, D)
    2 No

    A. What are the benefits? (CODE AS MANY AS APPLY)
       1–1 Reduce property damage
       1–2 Reduce illness
       1–3 Reduce injury
       1–4 Reduce deaths
       1–5 Enhance quality of life

       1–8 Other (specify) _____

    B. What proportion of the story is devoted to benefits?
       1 Less than ¼
       2 ¼–½
       3 ½–¾
       4 More than ¾

    C. Does story mention ratio of risk (cost) to benefit?
       1 Yes (answer A1)
       2 No

    A1. According to story, what is ratio?
       1 Benefits outweigh costs
       2 Benefits equal costs
       3 Costs outweigh benefits
       8 D.K.; conflicting opinions, etc.

    D. According to story, who is responsible for benefits of hazard? (CODE AS MANY AS APPLY)
       1–1 Victim
       1–2 Other individual (specify) _____
       1–3 Social category (e.g., women, homosexuals) (specify)

       _____
       1–4 Business, industry
       1–5 Doctors, medicine
       1–6 Government
       1–7 God, nature
       1–8 Other (specify) _____
       1–9 D.K.; no explicit or implicit mention of blame or responsibility (Skip to Q. 11)

A. (If more than one) Which of these is most important? Use one of codes 1–8, above; 9 = D.K.; no indication of which is most important; 0 = conflicting opinions about who is responsible.

B. Is the blame explicit or implicit in the story?
   1 Explicit
   2 Implicit

11. Does the story mention any alternatives (substitutes) for the materials hazard?
   1 Yes (answer A, B)
   2 No

A. What are the alternatives? CODE AS MANY AS APPLY.
   1–2 Change in lifestyle, activity
   1–4 Other materials hazard
   1–5 Energy hazard
   1–6 Complex technology

   1–8 Other (specify) _____

B. According to story
   1 Materials hazard in question is preferable to alternative (answer B1)
   2 Alternative hazard is preferable to materials hazard (answer B1)
   3 No preference; critical/skeptical of all
   8 Neutral or can't tell

B1. Why is that (according to story)?
   1 More benefits
   2 Fewer costs
   3 More benefits and fewer costs

   4 Other (specify) _____

12. Does the story explicitly mention any of the following social categories as being affected by the materials hazard? (ANSWER A, B, C, D, E)

A. Gender
   1 Yes, mentioned (answer A1)
   2 No

A1. According to story, who is affected by the materials hazard—
   1 Primarily men
   2 Primarily women
   3 Both equally

B. Race
   1 Yes, mentioned (answer B1)
   2 No

Codeform   7

B1. According to story, who is affected by the materials hazard—
    1 Primarily whites
    2 Primarily blacks
    3 Primarily other (specify) _____
    4 No differences by race

C. Age
    1 Yes, mentioned (answer C1)
    2 No

C1. According to story, who is affected by the materials hazard—
    1 Primarily children (under 18)
    2 Primarily young adults (19–30)
    3 Primarily middle-aged (31–55)
    4 Primarily older adults (56 +)
    5 No age differences

D. Class
    1 Yes, mentioned (answer D1)
    2 No

D1. According to story, who is affected by the materials hazard—
    1 Primarily middle-class
    2 Primarily working-class
    3 Primarily poor
    4 No class differences

E. Occupation
    1 Yes, mentioned (answer E1)
    2 No

E1. According to story, who is affected by the materials hazard—
    1 Primarily certain categories of worker (specify)

    _____

    2 No differences by occupation

13. What is the referent of the story (i.e., whose risk is emphasized?)
    1 Individual(s)
    2 Social category (e.g., women, yuppies) (specify)

    _____

    3 Community (answer A)

A. Is community—
    1 Narrow (e.g., neighborhood)
    2 Intermediate (e.g., city, state)
    3 Wide (country, world)
    8 D.K. or more than one type of referent

14. According to story, how does the risk get activated?
    1 Human error, failure, or neglect
    2 Mechanical failure (structural defect)
    3 Known experimental situation (primarily complex technology)
    4 Deliberate risk-taking (primarily activities)
    5 Nature, God (only if explicitly mentioned)
    9 DNA; no indication of how risk gets activated

    8 Other (specify) _____

15. According to story, who is blamed (held responsible) for disaster/hazard? (CODE AS MANY AS APPLY)
    1–1 Victim
    1–2 Other individual (specify) _____
    1–3 Social category (e.g., women, homosexuals) (specify)

    _____

    1–4 Business, industry
    1–5 Doctors, medicine
    1–6 Government
    1–7 God, nature
    1–8 Other (specify) _____
    1–9 D.K.; no explicit or implicit mention of blame or responsibility (Skip to Q. 16)

  A. (If more than one) Which of these is most important? Use one of codes 1–8, above; 9 = D.K.; no indication of which is most important; 0 = conflicting opinions about who is responsible _____

  B. Is the blame explicit or implicit in the story?
    1 Explicit
    2 Implicit

16. According to story, who is responsible for taking precautions against disaster/hazard? (CODE AS MANY AS APPLY)
    1–1 Victim
    1–2 Other individual (specify) _____
    1–3 Social category (e.g., women, homosexuals) (specify)

    _____

    1–4 Business, industry
    1–5 Doctors, medicine
    1–6 Government
    1–7 God, nature
    1–8 Other (specify) _____
    1–9 D.K.; no explicit or implicit mention of blame or responsibility (Skip to Q. 17)

25. Does story mention <u>conflicting</u> opinions about:

		Y	N
a.	Likelihood that hazard will occur	1	2
b.	Riskiness of the hazard (i.e., the likelihood that if it occurs, it will cause harm)	1	2
c.	Possibility or adequacy of precautions against the hazard	1	2
d.	Responsibility for hazard, or for taking precautions against it	1	2
e.	Benefits of hazard	1	2
f.	Benefits or costs of alternatives	1	2
g.	Anything else (specify) _____	1	2

26. Does story give any indication of how much weight to give different opinions, if conflicting opinions are mentioned?
    1 Yes (answer A, B)
    2 No
    8 DNA; no conflicting opinions mentioned

    A. How does story communicate what weight is to be given to a position? By adjectives, direct recommendations, difference in space or prominence, or what? (Code YES or NO for each)

		Y	N
(1)	By adjectives used?	1	2
(2)	By direct recommendations?	1	2
(3)	By difference in space for different opinions	1	2
(4)	By difference in prominence for different opinions	1	2
(5)	Other media (specify) _____	1	2

    B. Summarize the conflict and the position favored by the media. (If no position favored, just code "9" below)

    _____

    _____

    9 No position favored; "balanced" presentation

27. Does the story contain any action recommendations?
    1 Yes (answer A, B)
    2 No

    A. About what?

		Y	N
a.	Prevention of hazard	1	2
b.	Relief for hazard victims	1	2
c.	Further research	1	2
d.	Anything else (what?) _____	1	2

B. To whom are the recommendations addressed? (CODE AS MANY AS APPLY)
- 1–1   Reader/viewer
- 1–2   Government officials (other than scientists)
- 1–3   Scientists
- 1–4   Business/industry (including scientists)

- 1–8   Other (specify) _____

28. In your opinion, is the hazard/risk <u>portrayed</u> as fear-arousing, or not?
- 1   Yes (answer A)
- 2   No

A. What techniques are used to portray hazard/risk as fear-arousing?

		Y	N
1	Uses fear-arousing adjectives, metaphors (specify) _____	1	2
2	Gives more space to discussion of risks than to discussion of benefits or reassurance	1	2
3	Gives more prominence to discussion of risks than to discussion of benefits or reassurance	1	2
4	Gives more quotes from sources who emphasize costs rather than benefits or reassurance	1	2
5	Gives more prominence to quotes from sources who emphasize costs rather than benefits or reassurance	1	2
6	Other (specify) _____ _____	1	2

29. Does the story mention any other materials hazards?
- 1   Yes (answer A, B)
- 2   No

A. Which ones? (Names and 3-digit codes, if we have them; otherwise, 999 = no code)

_____   _____

_____   _____

B. Does one of these hazards lead to or result from the hazard that has been coded in this section?
- 1   Yes
- 2   No, no "causal chain"

Appendix C
News Stories and Scientific Articles on Which Accuracy Analysis Is Based

NEWS STORY/SCIENTIFIC ARTICLE

Case No.

#0151 "Jim Fixx was the man who convinced many of us that running was a way to better health." "ABC World News Tonight," Oct. 3, 1984.

David S. Siscovick et al., "The Incidence of Primary Cardiac Arrest During Vigorous Exercise." *New England Journal of Medicine* 311 (Oct. 4, 1984): 874–877.

#0153 "The *New England Journal* tonight published a landmark study." "CBS Evening News," Oct. 3, 1984.

Same source as in #0151.

#0156 "Also on this program tonight: Does heavy exercise prevent heart attacks or bring them on?" "NBC Nightly News," Oct. 9, 1984.

#0180 "There is still much to be learned about Acquired Immune Deficiency Syndrome, or AIDS." "NBC Nightly News," Oct. 9, 1984.

Jerome E. Groopman et al., "HTLV-III in Saliva of People with AIDS-Related Complex and Healthy Homosexual Men at Risk for AIDS," *Science* Oct. 26, 1984, pp. 447–448.

#0185 "This week's issue of the *American Medical Association Journal* is completely devoted to alcohol abuse in this country." "ABC World News Tonight," Oct. 11, 1984.

James L. Mills et al., "Maternal Alcohol Consumption and Birth Weight: How Much Alcohol Is Safe?" *Journal of the American Medical Association* 252 (Oct. 12, 1984): 1875–1879.

#0188 "A new study concludes today that for pregnant women taking even one or two alcoholic drinks a day can endanger the health of a child." "CBS Evening News," Oct. 11, 1984.

Same source as in #0185.

#0190 "Pregnant women got a strong new warning today about alcohol." "NBC Nightly News," Oct. 11, 1984.

Same source as in #0185.

#0301 "Turns out that about 30 percent of all heart attacks are silent attacks, so-called." "NBC Nightly News," Oct. 31, 1984.

William B. Kannel and Robert D. Abbott, "Incidence and Prognosis of Unrecognized Myocardial Infarction," *New England Journal of Medicine* 311 (No. 18, 1984): 1144–1147.

#1074 "Auxiliary Dam Is Being Built to Contain Mississippi River," *New York Times*, Sept. 2, 1984, p. 61.

Raphaal G. Kazmann and David B. Johnson, "If the Old River Control Structure Fails?" *Bulletin #12*. Report published by Louisiana Water Resources Research Institute, Louisiana State University, Baton Rouge, Sept. 1980.

#1144 Lawrence K. Altman, "Alzheimer's Disease Linked to Damaged Areas of Brain," *New York Times*, Sept. 7, 1984, p. 1.

Bradley T. Hyman, "Alzheimer's Disease: Cell-Specific Pathology Isolates the Hippocampal Formation," *Science* 225 (Sept. 14, 1984): 1168–1170.

Elizabeth M. Sajdel-Sulkowska and Charles A. Marotta, "Alzheimer's Disease Brain: Alterations in RNA Levels and in a Ribonuclease-Inhibitor Complex," *Science* 225 (Aug. 31, 1984): 947–948.

#1455 "High Cancer Risk Found in Siblings." *New York Times*, Sept. 20, 1984, p. B18.

Jacqueline Farwell and John T. Flannery, "Cancer in Relatives of Children with Central-Nervous-System Neoplasms," *New England Journal of Medicine* 311 (Sept. 20, 1984): 749–753.

#1617 Anastasia Toufexis, "Linking Drugs to the Dinner Table." *Time,* Sept. 24, 1984, p. 77.

Scott D. Holmberg et al., "Drug-Resistant Salmonella from Animals Fed Antimicrobials," *New England Journal of Medicine* 311 (Sept. 6, 1984): 617–622.

#1622 "Health Care Today: Teen Years Are Critical in Smoking Habit," *Amsterdam News,* Sept. 22, 1984, p. 20.

Nancy C. Doyle, "Smoking—A Habit That Should Be Broken," *Public Affairs Pamphlet No. 573A,* 1979, 1984.

#2036 Judith Randal, "1 in 5 Needs a Psychiatrist, Survey Reports," *New York Daily News,* Oct. 3, 1984, p. 39.

Archives of General Psychiatry 41 (Oct. 1984): 931–989 (several articles).

#2040 Harold M. Schmeck, Jr., "Almost One in 5 May Have Mental Disorder," *New York Times,* Oct. 3, 1984, p. 1.

Same source as in #2036.

#2043 "Study Warns Surgeons to Wait on Bypass," *New York Times,* Oct. 3, 1984, p. 19.

W. Linda Cashin et al., "Accelerated Progression of Atherosclerosis in Coronary Vessels with Minimal Lesions That Are Bypassed." *New England Journal of Medicine* 311 (Sept. 27, 1984): 824–828.

#2055 "Strenuous Exercise Reduces Heart Attack Risk, Study Says," *New York Times,* Oct. 4, 1984, p. 22.

Same source as in #0151.

#2060 Jerry E. Bishop, "Chances of Sudden Death Rise During Vigorous Activity, According to Study of Men," *Wall Street Journal,* Oct. 4, 1984, p. 1, 8.

Same source as in #0151.

#2096 Sharon Begley, "California's 'No Fault' Fault," *Newsweek,* Oct. 15, 1984, p. 111.

Kerry E. Sieh and Richard H. Jahns, "Holocene Activity of the San Andreas Fault at Wallace Creek, California," *Geological Society of America Bulletin* 95 (Aug. 1984): 883–896.

Kerry E. Sieh, "Lateral Offsets and Revised Dates of Large Prehistoric Earthquakes at Pallett Creek, Southern California," *Journal of Geophysical Research* 89 (Sept. 10, 1984): 7641–7670.

Caltech Newsbureau News Release, "San Andreas Fault Yielding Its Secrets," Sept. 24, 1984.

#2190 Judith Randal, "Study: Healthy Carriers May Be Spreading AIDS," *New York Daily News*, Oct. 19, 1984, p. 12.

Jerome E. Groopman et al., "HTLV-III in Saliva of People with AIDS-Related Complex and Healthy Homosexual Men at Risk for AIDS," *Science*, October 26, 1984, pp. 447–448.

David D. Ho et al., "HTLV-III in the Semen and Blood of a Healthy Homosexual Man," *Science*, October 26, 1984, pp. 451–452.

#2224 Matt Clark with Mariana Gosnell, "Alzheimer's: A New Promise," *Newsweek*, Oct. 29, 1984, p. 97.

Robert E. Harbaugh et al., "Preliminary Report: Intracranial Cholinergic Drug Infusion in Patients with Alzheimer's Disease," *Neurosurgery* 15 (1984): 514–517.

#2251 "Breakthrough: Hepatitis Virus Detected," *Time*, Nov. 5, 1984.

Belinda Seto et al., "Detection of Reverse Transcriptase Activity in Association with the Non-A, Non-B Hepatitis Agent(s)," *The Lancet*, Oct. 27, 1984, pp. 941–943.

#2295 Gerald F. Seib, "Israel, 4 Other Nations Seen Most Likely to Start Testing or Making Nuclear Arms," *Wall Street Journal*, Oct. 29, 1984, p. 36.

Warren H. Donnelly, "An Assessment of the Proliferation Threat of Today and Tomorrow and Replies to Questions Asked by Senator William Proxmire," Congressional Research Service, Sept. 24, 1984.

#2519 Marilyn Chase, "Researchers Report Headway in Treating Side Effect of AIDS," *Wall Street Journal*, Nov. 1, 1984, p. 43.

Jeffrey A. Golden et al., "Pneumocystis carinii Pneumonia Treated with alpha-Difluoromethylornithine," *The Western Journal of Medicine*, Nov. 1984, pp. 613–622.

#2792 "Health Care Today: Spend Funds on Research," *Amsterdam News*, Nov. 24, 1984, p. 22.

"A Study of American Attitudes toward Selected Smoking Issues and American Cancer Society Anti-Smoking Activities," Survey for the Tobacco Institute by the Roper Organization, Inc., Nov. 1984.

#2981 Harold M. Schmeck, Jr., "Researcher Finds Chromosome Weak Spots," *New York Times*, Nov. 30, 1984, p. B10.

Jorge J. Yunis and A. Lee Soreng, "Constitutive Fragile Sites and Cancer," *Science* 226 (Dec. 7, 1984): 1199–1203.

#2983   "Scientists may have found weak spots in human genes," *Wall Street Journal*, Nov. 30, 1984, p. 1.

Same source as in #2981.

#3034   Charles Leerhsen with Susan Katz, "The AMA Tries to KO Boxing," *Newsweek*, Dec. 17, 1984, p. 67.

Council on Scientific Affairs, "Brain Injury in Boxing," *Journal of the American Medical Association* 249 (Jan. 14, 1983): 254–257.

Donald J. Ross et al., "Boxers—Computed Tomography, EEG, and Neurological Evaluation," *Journal of the American Medical Association* 249 (Jan. 14, 1983): 211–213.

#3143   Daniel Goleman, "Schizophrenia: Early Signs Found," *New York Times*, Dec. 11, 1984, p. C1.

Norman Watt, ed., *Children at Risk for Schizophrenia*, New York: Cambridge University Press, 1984.

#3272   Natalie Angier, "Debate over a Frozen Planet," *Time*, Dec. 24, 1984, p. 56.

Committee on the Atmospheric Effects of Nuclear Explosions, *The Effects on the Atmosphere of a Major Nuclear Exchange*. Washington, D.C.: National Research Council, National Academy Press, 1985.

#3294   "Drug Blocks Virus Linked to AIDS, Researchers Report," *Wall Street Journal*, Dec. 21, 1984, p. 6.

Joseph B. McCormick et al., "Ribavirin Suppresses Replication of Lymphadenopathy-Associated Virus in Cultures of Human Adult T-Lymphocytes," *The Lancet*, Dec. 15, 1984, pp. 1367–1369.

#3301   Matt Clark with Deborah Witherspoon, "Still Too Many Caesareans?" *Newsweek*, Dec. 31, 1984, p. 70.

Norbert Gleicher, "Caesarean Section Rates in the United States," *Journal of the American Medical Association* 252 (December 21, 1984): 3273–3276.

#4302   "Doomsday in 2026 AD," *Time*, Nov. 14, 1960, p. 89.

Heinz von Foerster, Patricia M. Mora, and Lawrence W. Amiot, "Doomsday: Friday, 13 November, AD 2026," *Science* (Nov. 4, 1960): 1291–1295.

#4311   "Doctors on Sport," *Time*, Dec. 12, 1960, p. 75.

Thomas E. Shaffer et al., "The Child in Athletics," and Gyula J. Erdelyi, "Women in Athletics," *Proceedings of the Second Annual Conference on the Medical Aspects of Sports*. Washington, D.C.: American Medical Association, 1961, pp. 48–50, 59–63.

#4435 "Scientists Learning from Chilean Quake," *New York Times,* Dec. 16, 1960, p. 16.

C. Martin Duke, "The Chilean Earthquake of May 1960," *Science* 132 (Dec. 16, 1960): 1797–1802.

#9609 "The Pill's Eclipse," *Time,* Dec. 17, 1984, p. 79.

William D. Mosher and Christine A. Bachrach, "Contraceptive Use, United States, 1982." Data from the National Survey of Family Growth, *Vital and Health Statistics,* Series 23, No. 12, U.S. Department of Health and Human Services, NCHS, September 1986. DHHS Publication No. (PHS)86-1988.

#9654 "Study Says by 1990 Blacks Will Be Poorer," *Amsterdam News,* Dec. 22, 1984, p. 1.

Emanuel Tobier, *The Changing Face of Poverty: Trends in New York City 1960–1990.* New York: Community Service Society, 1984.

#9656 "Rich Man, Poor Man," *Wall Street Journal,* Nov. 28, 1984, p. 30.

Greg J. Duncan, *Years of Poverty, Years of Plenty: The Changing Economic Fortunes of American Workers and Families.* Ann Arbor, MI: Institute for Social Research, Survey Research Center, 1984.

#9729 "In what's being called a 'staggering exploit,' American and British scientists have reproduced the human gene that makes blood clot." "CBS Evening News," Nov. 11, 1984.

John J. Toole et al., "Molecular Cloning of a cDNA Encoding Human Antihaemophilic Factor," *Nature* 312 (Nov. 22, 1984): 342–347.

#9741 "Report Disputes Tying Exercise to Resistance," *New York Times,* Nov. 16, 1984, p. 23.

Harvey B. Simon, "The Immunology of Exercise," *Journal of the American Medical Association* 252 (Nov. 16, 1984): 2735–2738.

#9757 John Corey with others, "The Comforts of Home," *Newsweek,* Nov. 26, 1984, p. 96.

Gigliola Baruffi et al., "Patterns of Obstetric Procedures Use in Maternity Care," *Obstetrics and Gynecology* 64 (Oct. 1984): 493–498.

#9807 "When President Reagan sits down with Andrei Gromyko in a couple of weeks, an awful lot of Americans are going to be pleased." "NBC Nightly News," Sept. 13, 1984.

Daniel Yankelovich, "The Public Mood," *Foreign Affairs* (Fall 1984): 33–46.

ACCURACY CODE FORM

1. Case ID (4 cols.)

2. Type of Hazard
    1   Natural
    2   Activities
    3   Energy
    4   Materials
    5   Complex
    6   Illness

2A. No. of source stories on which news story is based (1, 2, 3, etc.)

3. How many statements of fact in the news story are based on the origi-
    nal source?
    1   1–3
    2   4–6
    3   7–10
    4   11–15
    5   16–20
    6   21 or more

3A. How many of these statements are substantially different from those
    in the original research report? (01, 02, 03, etc.)

3B. Give examples of the ways in which they differ.

3C. Not substantially different, but MORE precise than in original? 1–yes;
    2–no

3D. Not substantially different, but LESS precise than in original? 1–yes;
    2–no

3E. Not substantially different, but state fact in (transformed) *equivalent*
    form? 1–yes; 2–no

GIVE EXAMPLES:

1

4. Are there any statements of fact in the news report for which there is no source in the original research report?
    1 Yes (Answer A)
    2 No (Skip to Q. 5)
          (If yes) Give examples

A. Is any other source given for those statements?
    1 Yes, for all (answer B)
    2 Yes, for some (answer B)
    3 No

B. What is the source? (Check as many as apply)
    1 Interview with author or other scientist
    1 Other interview
    1 Other journal article
    1 Other (specify)

5. Is emphasis faithful to original?
    1 Yes
    2 No (Answer A)

A. (If no): Does news story—
    1 Portray hazard as more risky than original? (specify)
    2 Portray hazard as less risky (less harmful) than original? (specify)
    3 Portray hazard as more beneficial (or beneficial sooner) than original? (specify)
    4 Other (specify)

6. Does news story omit any important results?
    1 Yes
    2 No
        (If yes, which?)

7. Does news story omit any qualifying statements?
    1 Yes
    2 No
        (If yes, which?)

2

8. Does news story have a misleading/inaccurate headline? (For TV, use lead sentence)
    1 Yes
    2 No
    (If yes, specify how it's misleading and give headline

9. Does news story overstate the generalizability of the findings?
    1 Yes
    2 No
    (If yes: How?)

10. Does the news story treat speculations as facts?
    1 Yes
    2 No
    (If yes, explain)

11. Does news story contain information on methods:
    (1) Complete: all details included
    (2) Partial but adequate: all essential details included
    (3) Partial but inadequate: some essential details omitted
    (4) No information on methods at all
    (5) Some information about methods is erroneous (Give example)

12. Any supporting comments on research from other sources?
    1 Yes (Specify: Who? Any studies cited?)
    2 No

13. Any conflicting/challenging comments from other sources?
    1 Yes (Specify: Who? Any studies cited?)
    2 No

14. Any qualifying comments from other sources?
    1 Yes (Specify: Who? Any studies cited? Reason for qualification?)
    2 No

15. Is the original source:
    1 Peer-reviewed
    2 Other journal
    3 Book
    4 Other (specify)
    5 Not a published source

16. Is any related research cited in the news story?
    1 Yes (Answer A)
    2 No

    A. Is the research published?
        1 Yes
        2 No
        8 DK

17. Byline
    1 Byline (including anchor and reporter)
    2 Wire service
    3 Editorial; column
    8 No byline

18. Media
    1 Newspaper
    2 TV
    3 Newsmagazine

4

Index